# Cut it short: DIY early retirement plan

Patrick Nguyen

2023

2

# Contents

**1 Preliminaries**   **5**
    1.1 In this chapter . . . . . . . . . . . . . . . . . . 6
    1.2 About you and me . . . . . . . . . . . . . . . 7
          1.2.1 Me . . . . . . . . . . . . . . . . . . . . . 7
          1.2.2 You . . . . . . . . . . . . . . . . . . . . 8
    1.3 What is retirement and why retire? . . . . . . 9
          1.3.1 What retirement is not . . . . . . . . 9
          1.3.2 What retirement is . . . . . . . . . . 10
          1.3.3 Goal: the happy ever after . . . . . . 11
    1.4 Designing The Master Plan . . . . . . . . . . 12
          1.4.1 Finance, health, and purpose . . . . 12
          1.4.2 Sustainability . . . . . . . . . . . . . 13
          1.4.3 Methodology . . . . . . . . . . . . . 17
          1.4.4 Failure modes . . . . . . . . . . . . . 20
          1.4.5 Has the time come? . . . . . . . . . . 20
    1.5 The rest of this book . . . . . . . . . . . . . . 21
    1.6 Summary . . . . . . . . . . . . . . . . . . . . 23
    1.7 Reading further . . . . . . . . . . . . . . . . 24

**2 Finance**   **25**
    2.1 In this chapter . . . . . . . . . . . . . . . . . . 25

|  |  |  |
|---|---|---|
| 2.2 | Bad things happen | 26 |
|  | 2.2.1 Taxonomy and cycles | 27 |
|  | 2.2.2 Some vignettes | 36 |
|  | 2.2.3 Consequences | 43 |
|  | 2.2.4 Thriving | 52 |
| 2.3 | Classical financial planning | 57 |
|  | 2.3.1 Framework | 57 |
|  | 2.3.2 Spend in retirement | 59 |
|  | 2.3.3 Withdrawal amount | 61 |
|  | 2.3.4 Portfolio allocation | 63 |
|  | 2.3.5 Mitigation strategies | 67 |
| 2.4 | Buffer strategy | 68 |
|  | 2.4.1 Outline | 68 |
|  | 2.4.2 It rarely matters greatly | 69 |
|  | 2.4.3 Joint stock ownership | 74 |
|  | 2.4.4 The delivery problem: maturity mismatch | 81 |
|  | 2.4.5 Strategy | 82 |
| 2.5 | Summary | 89 |
| 2.6 | Reading further | 91 |
|  | 2.6.1 Resilience | 91 |
|  | 2.6.2 Sea change | 93 |
|  | 2.6.3 Mechanics | 106 |
|  | 2.6.4 Economics and finance | 113 |

## 3 Health    121

| | | |
|---|---|---|
| 3.1 | In this chapter | 121 |
| 3.2 | Goal: actuarial or actual years | 122 |
| 3.3 | In the long run | 124 |
|  | 3.3.1 Suffer then die | 124 |
|  | 3.3.2 From Galen to Pasteur | 126 |

|  |  | 3.3.3 Outlook . . . . . . . . . . . . . . . 127 |
|---|---|---|

- 3.4 Grooming physical health . . . . . . . . . 130
  - 3.4.1 Evaluation metrics . . . . . . . . . 131
  - 3.4.2 Sleep . . . . . . . . . . . . . . . . . 134
  - 3.4.3 Nutrition . . . . . . . . . . . . . . 135
  - 3.4.4 Body training . . . . . . . . . . . . 137
  - 3.4.5 Unexpected infirmity . . . . . . . . 138
- 3.5 Mental health . . . . . . . . . . . . . . . . 138
  - 3.5.1 Evaluation . . . . . . . . . . . . . . 139
  - 3.5.2 Intervention . . . . . . . . . . . . . 140
- 3.6 Summary . . . . . . . . . . . . . . . . . . 140
- 3.7 Reading further . . . . . . . . . . . . . . . 142

## 4 Purpose     149
- 4.1 In this chapter . . . . . . . . . . . . . . . 149
- 4.2 Goal design . . . . . . . . . . . . . . . . . 150
  - 4.2.1 Confounding factors . . . . . . . . 151
  - 4.2.2 A life worth living . . . . . . . . . 154
  - 4.2.3 Success is happiness . . . . . . . . 157
  - 4.2.4 Desirable properties . . . . . . . . 159
- 4.3 Buddhism . . . . . . . . . . . . . . . . . . 164
  - 4.3.1 Enthymemes . . . . . . . . . . . . . 165
  - 4.3.2 Process . . . . . . . . . . . . . . . 168
  - 4.3.3 Dangers . . . . . . . . . . . . . . . 171
- 4.4 Summary . . . . . . . . . . . . . . . . . . 173
- 4.5 Reading further . . . . . . . . . . . . . . . 175

## 5 My Master Plan     185
- 5.1 Finance . . . . . . . . . . . . . . . . . . . 186
  - 5.1.1 Accumulation phase . . . . . . . . 186
  - 5.1.2 Steady state . . . . . . . . . . . . . 188

|     |       |                                |
| --- | ----- | ------------------------------ |
|     | 5.1.3 | Where we are in 2023 ....... 189 |
|     | 5.1.4 | Armageddon ............. 193   |
|     | 5.1.5 | Legacy ................. 196   |
| 5.2 | Health ....................... 197 | |
| 5.3 | Purpose ...................... 198 | |
|     | 5.3.1 | Goal ................... 198   |
|     | 5.3.2 | Process ................. 202  |
|     | 5.3.3 | Schedule ................ 204  |
| 5.4 | Retrospective ................. 206 | |
|     | 5.4.1 | Unexpected consequences ..... 206 |
|     | 5.4.2 | Finance ................. 207  |
|     | 5.4.3 | Milestones ............... 209 |
|     | 5.4.4 | Tyranny of lists ........... 210 |
| 5.5 | Epilogue ..................... 212 | |

# Chapter 1

# Preliminaries

Hello and welcome to my retirement planning book! I am thrilled and honored to capture your attention for a little while.

This book is about planning for early retirement based on my experience as an engineer. As such, it doesn't give you an exact plan, because such a plan would need to be customized according to your preferences and specific circumstances. It offers a guide on how to think about planning for retirement, in a concise format that you can implement with minimal time. Life in the grinder can be busy, and it's hard to look up and think outside the box – whether you'll decide to continue on your current path or take a turn, after you finish this book, you'll be able to make that choice with confidence. Remember, I am offering you a mental framework to approach the problem, and you're in charge.

By and large, chapters and sections in this book are self-contained, so feel free to read them in the order that you like, or skip some altogether.

Let's get started!

> **Diamonds and pebbles.** Occasionally, you will find random thoughts or quotes such as this one. They have a special indent. They contain no essential information and you can safely skip them. They are meant to entertain. You might treasure some as diamonds and discard others as pebbles.

## 1.1 In this chapter

First, we want to lay down the preliminaries that will frame the rest of the discussion. We'll start with getting to know each other first to see where we have compatible profiles. This will tell you where I'm coming from, as well as understand where you fit in the intended audience of the book. Some passages will speak directly to you, and in some others, you will think my models primitive.

Then, we'll need to define in broad terms what retirement actually entails. For the majority of individuals approaching retirement, it is a vague notion of some pleasant state in the far-off future. We need to make that a tangible reality, because, believe or not, you still eat, sleep, and get bored in retirement.

Once we've narrowed down our goal, we need to get ready for planning. What sets this book apart from others on retirement is that it is meant for people who retire early, and the time horizon opens up a universe of possibilities.

The complexity requires a bit more of a methodical approach. Planning is not only about preparing for retiring and retirement, but also about helping you decide when (or if) you will retire.

Once we've laid out these foundations, we'll introduce the three cornerstones of finance, health and purpose that underpin the plan.

## 1.2 About you and me

Just so that we're on the same page, let's introduce ourselves so that we know where we come each from.

### 1.2.1 Me

> **Singleminded focus.** Itzhak Perlman was one of the top violinists in his generation. Approached by a writer about a biography, he shot the idea down: "My first violin at age 5. First recital aged 10. And I've been playing ever since. That's all." I discovered automatic speech recognition in 1996 during an internship and it has been my passion ever since.

I am not a philosopher, nutritionist, or economics professor. This book was written from my lived perspective. I am an engineer, a second- and first-generation immigrant, and celibate. I retired in late 2019, aged 44 (around the actuarial mid-life), after a 20-year career. I consistently worked more than 70-hour weeks, working all days of the week, taking little vacation, and loved most of it. I gave my career everything I had, yet some say I never worked a day in my life. Throughout this journey, I was unbelievably fortunate to have come into contact with truly exceptional people, in every dimensions of intelligence and character.

People said I would not last a day in retirement. I plotted my exit for years, slowly, with fear and trepidation, before bowing out. It's been three years now and counting.

It took a while for the ideas to congeal. The primary impulse of this book is to distill the result and create a shortcut for people in the same situation as I was prior to retirement. I'm talking to my younger self, as it were.

## 1.2.2 You

So, dear reader, let me describe how I think about you. You are about mid-life, say, in your forties or fifties. You are a professional who lives a full life – you have little time to devote to exploring radical changes in your life. You may be successful financially or filled with purpose in what you do most of the time. It feels like you could continue on your current path for decades longer. Yet a question beckons in the recesses of your mind – is there a better path?

You trust no one intellectually. You prefer informed, rational decisions. You want to review the process and implement the thinking framework on your own. You know better than to entrust one of the most important decisions in your life to a blog written by a twenty-something blogger who dropped out of an arts degree, or a generative AI summarizing the vast sea of mediocre advice. You seek to optimize well-being and want to feel reasonably comfortable that your plans will portage you safely until the end.

So you want to learn how to fish. Welcome, friend! Let's walk through the process of planning for voluntary early retirement. This book can be read in a day, but implementation will depend on your situation. You may do it sooner than you think.

## 1.3 What is retirement and why retire?

For most people, retirement is like a distant idea that is either repulsive or a pipe dream that will never become a reality, such as one's own death or the college graduation of one's children. It means different things to different people. The first step is to narrow down the idea, and, more importantly, reify the concept so that it becomes a clear and tangible goal. We're not going to plan every minute of every day in retirement, but we need to be able to picture it in our mind clearly to ensure that during that time, all needs and requisites are satisfied.

### 1.3.1 What retirement is not

**It is not rage quitting.** Let's be honest. We all had moment of despair a few times in our careers. Being passed over for a promotion or realizing that we made a big mistake at work, and it feels like we're completely unfit for work and we should just give up. Quitting your job in a moment of rage or in the face of a temporary setback is not retirement. Retirement is not an escape where all your problems vanish. It's simply another way to use your time that you consider more worthwhile.

**It is not a cardiac arrest.** On the other end of the spectrum, there are those who believe that retirement is the ultimate failure, when one is no longer useful to society and condemned to wander aimlessly, disgraced, rudderless, inglorious and impotent, awaiting death. While in retirement you will relinquish the identity that has served you for most of your life, your time will be spent achieving different goals, that could be even more fruitful than the activity you're engaged in.

## 1.3.2 What retirement is

**The end of gainful employment.** By and large, the first major hurdle to retirement is to relinquish your job. Because the retirement period is long, this part implies a careful consideration of the feasibility of maintaining a desired lifestyle for several decades, based on current savings.

**The end of a social life.** If you spend 8 hours a day at the office, you'll make some friends there. The office is a great way to meet people with similar interest and a shared goal. You have to find other support networks, or, better yet, live as an island unto yourself.

**The end of your current identity.** You will also relinquish that grandiose epithet that you have toiled for decades to attain, Vice President of this or General Manager of that. The external markers of achievement and success will belong to the past.

**A life of leisure.** Happiness does mean that the urge to fulfill one's duty to use one's productive capacity is

## 1.3. WHAT IS RETIREMENT AND WHY RETIRE?

quenched. More on the purpose later.

### 1.3.3 Goal: the happy ever after

So, now let's imagine you are retired. What makes that a desirable state? First, it has to be final and sustainable. It's not retirement if you go back to work after a decade. Second, it has to be what you want to do (otherwise it would preferable to continue working).

Therefore, retirement should bring about a greater and sustainable happiness. This encompasses the apparent goals that people often confuse with retirement, such as financial independence, fulfilling one's destiny, etc. In a survey, participants were asked to provide a list of 10 things they wanted. Shockingly, fewer than 5% explicitly mentioned happiness (if memory serves). They confused the perceived means to achieve an undefined concept of happiness with the thing itself. We have to be clear about this: *happiness is success*. Money, fame, power do not equate success if you have a higher purpose in mind. If you should decide that money is happiness, then so be it, but not the other way around. You'll hear people say that they have to choose between happiness and success – this is nonsense. Finally, understand that we have not defined happiness thus far, but there is a semblance of a rational process that will help us define this mental state with better clarity under certain assumptions.

There you go. Now, we just need to figure out how to make a plan to reach the happy ever after. Simple, right?

## 1.4 Designing The Master Plan

Building a plan serves the following purposes:

1. Defining the goal

2. Identifying requisites for success

3. Identifying risk factors, failure modes and mitigation strategies

4. Developing a level of confidence of feasibility, and that the approach is comprehensive

5. Acquiring the intellectual means to correct course should unforeseen events occur

6. Understanding the best timing for the entry point (retiring)

Since this is a complex task, we will divide it up into three sub-tasks, each tackling a different aspect of the practicality of retirement. Each of these tasks has different risk factors and solutions. When all sub-tasks are completed, we know if requisites for retirement are met.

### 1.4.1 Finance, health, and purpose

As mentioned before, broadly speaking, happiness is the goal. Happiness is a mental phenomenon. It exists within the mind.

Part of retirement planning involves defining that happiness more precisely. We're going to do that by laying a few constraints (duty) and desired optimization functions

## 1.4. DESIGNING THE MASTER PLAN

(pleasure). Happiness means solving for pleasure by still fulfilling one's duty. That, we call **purpose**.

To ensure that the mind can fully enjoy the benefits of retirement unimpeded, it is best that we make sure that its encasing, the body, remains in proper condition for frictionless operation. The ability to move with grace and dignity, to live long, sleeping well and freedom from depression are all examples of a body well cared for. We call that **health**.

The body itself needs clothing, shelter, food, medicine, and additional props to satisfy the body and mind – perhaps a travel and gym budget. Generally speaking, money is credit for services rendered to the society, and to retire we must have secured enough credit to be cared for by the society for the remainder of our life. We call that **finance**.

Traditionally, you will see books about retirement addressing the aspect of finance exclusively. First, because it is relatively easy to define and second, because it is the one that requires the most time to setup. We will tackle this first, then move on to health and purpose. Although these aspects can sometimes impinge on each other (for example, a passion for bungee jumping may be purposeful but it is not healthy), it's reasonable to address them independently. Regardless of the choices made in each aspect, the range of expected worst-case outcomes is similar.

### 1.4.2 Sustainability

> **The river flows 30 years to the East, and it flows 30 years to the West.** With a 2000-year history, China has seen its share of changes. Over long periods of time, change is

expected. Which, we don't know. You have to find a core of resilient behaviors to accommodate various possibilities. The Yangtze river is still flowing in the same direction today.

Perhaps the distinguishing feature for this book is that it is aiming at people retiring earlier in life. Rather than provisioning for a 20 years horizon of slower pace of life, we are contemplating a longer potential life span of 50 years. The phrase "I'd never thought I'd see the day" takes on a different meaning. You will most certainly see a lot of things in your remaining time, *inshallah*. Many of them will go right, many of them will go wrong, and they're not the ones that are cause for concern. It's the big things that go very, very wrong every now and then that we need to provision for.

The human mind tends to have difficulty imagining and estimating the likelihood of rare events. To illustrate this, let's consider a "calamity" – a stock market crash of more than 60%, the fall of the preeminent world power, a kinetic war between the largest world powers, or a pandemic – that you expect to occur approximately once every century. The following table illustrates the example of the assassination of a sitting US president. It's been three generations since the last successful assassination, so it seems like a forever forgone tradition, but we're actually much in line with the past.

## 1.4. DESIGNING THE MASTER PLAN

| Age of the American republic | 350 years |
|---|---|
| Number of sitting presidents assassinated | 4 |
| Time since founding without assassination | 90 years |
| ... until second assassination | 16 years |
| ... until third | 20 years |
| ... until last to date | 62 years |
| ... until today | 59 years |

Please note that we are measuring the duration between events. In queuing theory, they are called inter-arrival times. When all events have the same magnitude, duration and probability per annum are two sides of the same coin. This understanding is especially helpful when contemplating investments, particularly fixed income.

Misfortunes can happen with a long time between events, or within a shorter period. The following table summarizes, in rough terms, probabilities that a disastrous event might occur.

| A calamity happens at least once | Probability |
|---|---|
| ... within the next year | 1% |
| ... within 10 years | 10% |
| ... within 20 years | 20% |
| ... within 50 years | 40% |
| ... within 250 years | 90% |
| Any of 5 calamities ... within 50 years | 90% |

From the table, we see that you may get lucky over a span of 20 years, as indeed we have in the period of relative stability up to 2023. However, over a 50-year span, it is almost certain that something untoward will happen. Since 1970, we have witnessed a US default, gold expropriation, price controls, the fall of the second superpower, the rise of Japan (not a calamity), the Great Financial Crisis, a mild pandemic, two stock market drawdowns exceeding 40%, an oil price shock, and famines in various countries. Although it has been a very pleasant time, it is unlikely to continue for the next half century.

> **Long or fat.** Fat tails are probability distributions in which extreme outcomes are more likely than usual. During the financial crisis, a banker at a top investment bank blamed the failure of his investment strategy to a six-sigma event. That is, an event that would occur on average once every million years, about 5 times the duration of our species. Maybe, just maybe, his model was wrong. A variable with a long tail distribution exhibits very extreme events with non-negligible probability. The distribution of language is like that: you have to read an inordinate amount of books to encounter all words in the English language. Both are heavy tails, which means that irregular events are more likely than normal. The definitions are a bit fluid depending on whom you read.

Roughly speaking, something that occurs once every century has half a chance of happening again in a half century. Since 1922, the world has experienced a great depression, a world war, a cold war, nuclear events, famines, revolutions, hyperinflation in one of the most developed countries in the world, and a holocaust. Tens of millions have perished in famines and purges while birthing communism, and entire nations have been eradicated in the process. Bad things can happen. Nay, it's almost certain that a really, really

## 1.4. DESIGNING THE MASTER PLAN

bad thing will happen in the next half century. Any probability above, say, 30% is **as good as certain**, since it would be foolish not to consider it during planning.

So, how do we prepare for this?

### 1.4.3 Methodology

To plan further, we have to engage in an exercise of unraveling complexity. Not every minute of retirement can be planned. We just need to have enough to ensure that we have sufficient resources to initiate remedial actions should the need arise, regardless of *what happens*. Regrettably, there is no absolute guarantee that it will work, but we need to be able to say that we have thoroughly examined all factors and the risk-reward ratio is attractive.

We mostly focus on heavy tail risk factors. There are a few categories. There are natural causes, such as pandemics, earthquakes and tsunamis. There are man-made causes such as wars and revolutions. The following figure illustrates an example of disruptive risk factors and their consequences to us.

20                    CHAPTER 1. PRELIMINARIES

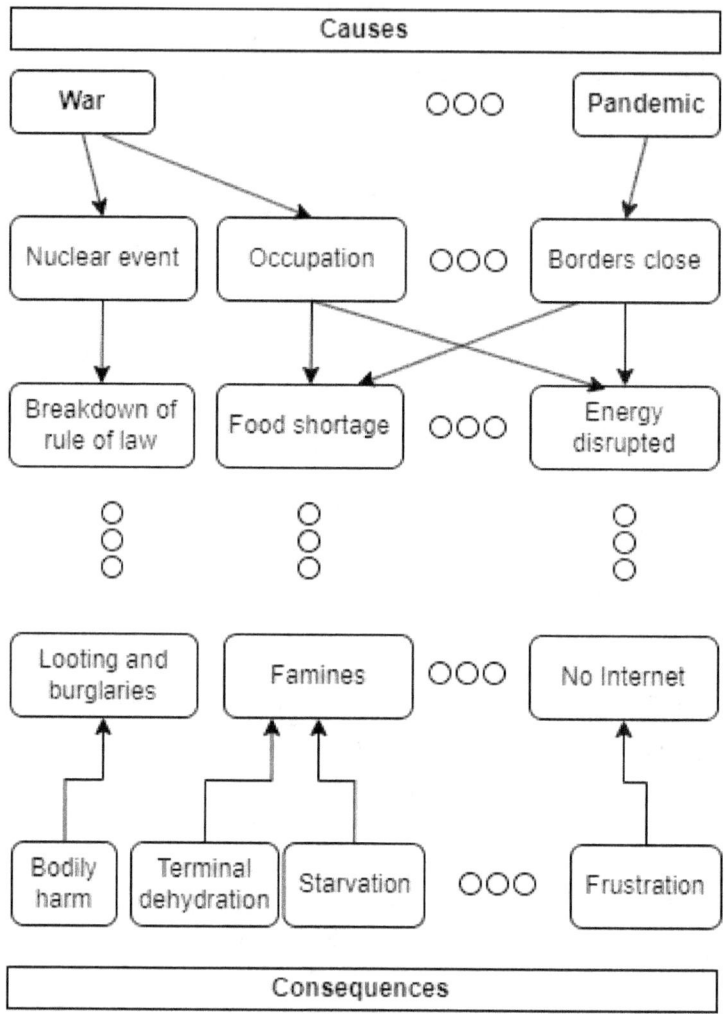

Following the figure, going top-down means starting from the causes and figuring out their implications for us. Bottom-up means identifying our basic needs and determining how to secure them in any condition. While the

## 1.4. DESIGNING THE MASTER PLAN

root causes are important and dictate the types of calamities that can occur, there is an unknowable web of complexities that determines how they will flow down to us. It is difficult to be confident that we have properly evaluated the probabilities, and whether we have a complete and comprehensive view of the events.

On the other hand, with some work, it is easier to contemplate our needs in retirement. These needs are the conditions for happiness, that mental phenomenon. We'll come back to that notion later, but for now, let us just note that the fewer needs or conditions for happiness, the more resilience we possess and the easier it is to plan. If we could be happy come rain or shine, planning would be rather simple. Starting from our needs, we can also gain an instinctive understanding of the costs and complexity required as we layer more and more desiderata. Therefore, we will work bottom-up. The constructive approach, rather than analytical, is both quick and effective.

Finally, nearly all complex systems, ranging from software to airplanes, typically commence with a prototype. Prototypes help identify issues and fix ideas hands-on. While I did not personally use this technique, I highly recommend retirement trials. Take a sabbatical between jobs of a few months to a year to get a feel of what happens. You may get some new ideas. Divorce frequently ensues when relationships undergo a rebalance, and the first cracks can often be spotted then.

Now that we've figured out that exogenous events may have adverse consequences, some more probable than others, it is best we rank them. While preparing for retirement, we need to start covering the basics first, and move to the frivolous last. We will draw a line when the effort is just not worth it: that's when we know we're ready to retire.

## 1.4.4 Failure modes

Because nothing is for certain, one has to contemplate the possibility that, despite our best intentions, an unwanted event will occur. Broadly speaking, there is a continuum between:

- you have more than enough money – you run out of money

- you live a long, healthy life – you die prematurely

- you are happy and content as never before – you don't want to continue

Every point on that continuum has a rough probability, and you must evaluate your tolerance for failure on each axis. You need to be comfortable with the level of risk you're taking. This is balanced against continuing on your current path, which carries its own risks and misery.

## 1.4.5 Has the time come?

When you retire, just like when you move to another job, it is essential to gauge the pros and cons. You may be sacrificing a pay package for the opportunity to accomplish something greater. With a difference: the inevitability of it. One day you will die, even on the job. You won't be able to carry your wealth, influence, or reputation with you.

So it's natural to start to be explicit about what you want to be written on your tombstone – a mission statement of sorts. Concretely, how would the phrase "a life worth living" apply to you? That is the **purpose** of retirement.

How long will it take to achieve? The inexorable decline in **health** will instill a sense of urgency in you. Youth is wasted on the young: a healthy body is required for many meaningful endeavors. Don't wait until it's too late.

Finally, can you afford to pull out of the labor force? The state of your **finances** will be the final obstacle to overcome.

The final purpose of the plan is to determine if the time has come for you to start another chapter in your life.

## 1.5 The rest of this book

Now we know how we're going to build up the plan, let's get on with it. That's what the rest of the book is about. We will be focusing on each of the concentric circles – finance, health, and purpose individually. We will modulate the approach for each of them: we will ponder about the goals, risk factors, upside, and solutions. Like this chapter, each chapter will have a section where you can find pointers for further reading. You can read the chapters out of order and skip chapters entirely.

In the first chapter, **Finance**, we will review some events from history. They will give us a flavor of the realm of possibilities that we need to protect against. There are cycles or secular trends that give these events some structure. For instance, contrarily to popular belief, high levels of inflation are not random occurrences like car accidents; rather, they resemble a dam breaking. The pressure gradually builds up along the cracks that have formed. The cracks build up until the dam breaks and a massive wave of destruction is unleashed. Proper planning is agnostic: to be prepared whatever happens, however, prioritizing based on likelihoods is expedient. Then, we'll take a look at classical financial advice. They have some value for different situations. They tend to be inappropriate for early retirement, but, on the whole, they are not catastrophically wrong. We will then introduce how to structure our investment portfolio.

In the second chapter, **Health**, we take a look at physical and mental well-being. We distinguish between life span (longevity) and health span (duration of healthy life). We should level set expectations: we don't believe the singularity will occur soon enough to rescue us. Healthy, happy living might extend our life span by no more than a decade, or just 20% to 25% of retirement. It is more important that we spend that time with the freedom and dignity that a well functioning body affords.

In the third chapter, **Purpose**, we study life goals – the grandiose goal of finding meaning in life. We take a constructive approach, starting with incontrovertible desired properties of the goal leading to the happy ever after. We must make certain reasonable assumptions and validate them along the path. The goal includes progress along the path, so no time is ever lost.

The last chapter concludes this book with my own master plan.

## 1.6 Summary

Well, I hope you found this first chapter engaging.

We got to know each other. We're looking at a short book for the busy, but do-it-yourself professional. We'll be targeting retirement from an angle of early retirement.

We crystallized the notion of retirement – essentially, the end of gainful employment – away from romantic notions of a permanent vacation or a miserable, inglorious slow death. The goal of retirement should be the happy ever after, but it does not happen automatically on its own.

This is where planning happens. Planning revolves around three facets: finance, health, and purpose. Each facet has its own chapter devoted to it. Early retirement is characterized by a need to think long-term sustainability. Fat tail, adverse events will occasionally sink our defenses. To prepare for these events, we survey the major causes, then proceed to work our way from the bottom by protecting our basic needs. We prioritize preparations by imagining the failure modes. By the end of the planning process, we should have a picture of whether we are ready for retirement. The time has come when retirement is a promotion, while we still have time to enjoy, and we have the necessary resources to sustain our desired lifestyle.

The book will continue by examining each of the facets: finance, health and purpose. Each chapter includes a section recommending further reading materials.

## 1.7 Reading further

**People say that life is the real thing, but I prefer reading.** When reading how things went wrong over the centuries, when life was nasty, brutish, and short, it's best to live those experiences vicariously. In fact, reading provides us with efficient access to a wide range of opinions, situations, and experiences that we would never be able to experience in the flesh.

Each chapter includes a list of books that I found interesting. Some of them are required reading. These books have the potential to save you from uncomfortable situations.

# Chapter 2

# Finance

Let's now shift our focus to securing material comfort in retirement. This will be the longest chapter, as this aspect is the one that is almost singularly studied in retirement preparations. And for good reason: for the majority of people, it acts as the most stringent gating function to retirement, and it is not well understood.

## 2.1 In this chapter

This chapter consists of three parts. First, bearing in mind that sustainability over half a century presents its own challenges, we examine major negative exogenous events that could occur. Pandemics and wars come to mind. We catalog them in time and type, then review their implications on our well-being.

Second, we review the state-of-the-art financial advice on retirement: goal, portfolio allocation and quick-and-dirty rules of the thumb. By and large, while they leave much to be desired on methodology, the resulting advice is not unreasonable. Tenets such as diversification and leaning on equity returns should be heeded.

Third, we offer our buffer strategy to secure income with some probability, come rain or shine. It does not offer tactical allocations, but it is a rough guideline on portfolio allocation in retirement.

## 2.2 Bad things happen

**The end of good times.** If anyone should know about bad things happening, my ancestry should know. After about a century or so under the same dynasty, Vietnam was colonized by France. The people navigated the French regime change until the monarchy fell half a century later. Soon after, the civil war began. There's nothing so bloody and cruel as a civil war. The losers were expropriated, sometimes tortured, and persecuted. Those who fled as boat people endured unspeakable villainy at the hands of Thai pirates. However, strangely, no one ever took me aside and warned me that bad things could happen. It's excruciating to remember, but an exogenous reminder could be harder still.

It's a fact of life: bad things happen. What kind of bad things happen? If they happen for a reason (especially man-made ones), is there rhyme or reason to when they

## 2.2. BAD THINGS HAPPEN

occur? What becomes of us when they do? We'd like to get a qualitative feel.

### 2.2.1 Taxonomy and cycles

Before we buy a safe for our guns, gold, and passports, let's first get a feel of what could happen. After all, if you get hit by an EMP, the electronic opening code wouldn't do you much good. If burglars come with guns, you may lose life and treasure.

We want to get a sense of what kind of situations would unfold when bad events occur. We would like to determine which events happen jointly. Events of the same type do not occur simultaneously, and cycles give a sequence in which events can occur. For instance, a devastatingly large meteorite will not collide with the earth at the same time as a comet would. The joint probability is vanishingly small. It's enough to consider the general type of anything large enough crashing into the earth. Furthermore, there is a causal chain whereby famines would cause unrest and competition for scarce resources and, in turn, war. Before the Thirty Years War, when potatoes were not available worldwide, wars would cause such a drain on resources that the conduct of agricultural affairs would be disrupted to such an extent that food would become scarce.

**The horsemen of the apocalypse**

It's fair to assume that all reasonably probable threats are of a kind that we have seen before. We're not terribly concerned about the end of the sun here, but asteroids hitting the Earth are fair game (spoiler: they don't matter anyway). It's moot to assign precise probabilities to them. There is a chain of action that leads to impact on your life that will usually give you from minutes to years to prepare. Many of these events will be global, and some will only affect your area or social position. Once again, the point of the exercise is not to precisely map out what will unfold, but to get a palette of the realm of possibilities.

**Leap to pole position.** The Shashoujian, usually translated as Assassin's mace, was a weapon that could break an opponent's blade, or their armor. It figures Chinese folklore of the antiquity. A cousin, the hand mace, was one of the 18 weapons of Gong Fu. It is said that General Xin Xiong in the Tang Dynasty wielded the weapon, with a secret skill passed down to him from generations. The term has been used in Chinese military doctrine, and its implications are debated. It is understood to be a weapon that can unexpectedly render current defenses or weaponry ineffectual, to allow a seemingly weaker adversary to win. Hypersonic missiles that circumvent the earth come to mind: they attack from the South, where the US has no defenses. Do not discount possibilities that a reversal of fortune could come out of left field and change the balance of military power quickly.

**Wars.** There are many different kinds of wars: asymmetric wars (state against terrorism), cold wars and trade wars, cyber wars, strategic wars (nuclear, space), and hot (or kinetic: good old fashioned bullet against bullet). At the heart of many wars lies a dispute about land or a resource (oil, granaries, diamonds). Most of the thinking on the conduct of war today tends to be a variation of von Clausewitz and de Jomini: first, war is a continuation of political objectives by other means. Second, we want to apply massive concentration of force until a specific aim is obtained (not always toppling the opposing regime). Finally, Chairman Mao's On Guerrilla Warfare and Trinquier's counter-insurgency in the French style of Algeria (minus the torture, perhaps) offer templates on how actors might approach asymmetric warfare. This applies to cases when your own government wants to put down rebellion, or when large enough communities want to reclaim the monopoly of violence from the state. In every case, it's a cataclysmically wasteful, unpleasant affair. There will be large-scale expropriation (capital controls, forced conversions of factories or resources), expedited para-judicial punishments, and massive destruction of resources. Violence can come swiftly, at unpredictable times, and there is no true safe place. Temporary or permanent disturbance of basic needs (water, food, shelter) can also occur.

**Biological events.** Whether man-made or from a random mutation, pestilence is a classic. The most devastating ones humans are the ones where the vector responsible for transmission is not humans, and where we are just unfortunate bystanders. The Black Death survived in rats and did not need humans to propagate. Waves of infection in Europe recurred for centuries. One day, either in a rogue lab or misguided large-scale drug or food experiment, we will cause massive casualties. Equally, we only have to look at the response to covid-19 to find clues at quickly governments can employ quarantine measures to suppress elections, the right to assemble, and track individual locations. Startlingly, Australia blocked her own citizens from entering the country, and Canada, hardly regarded of as the beacon of authoritarian rule, froze the bank accounts of anti-vaccine protesters. Remarkably, in a matter of months, we managed to develop new vaccines that attacked the spike protein, and coerced 70% of the population into getting inoculated. In the highly unlikely, but possible event that the spike protein proves essential for some critical biological pathway, we faced a near extinction level event to combat a very nasty flu. Massive disruptions in supply chains are to be expected. Trust in local communities can also break down, which destroys the very fabric of society. Sometimes, as when the plague struck indiscriminately, the rapid transfer of property between generations favored women, so it's not always all bad on the whole, but it could be bad for you.

**Civilization is two meals away from barbarism.** Imagine what would happen if food supply was disrupted. Most people keep about a week or two of supply of food at home. Everything could function normally for a short while. But when faced with starvation, it's likely that looting and violence would occur as people would fight over scarce resources. That could happen within a couple of weeks.

**Famines.** It would be easy to dismiss famines as a relic of the past. In the last handful of centuries, with the advent of

## 2.2. BAD THINGS HAPPEN

resistant crops such as the potato, nitrate-based fertilizers, and mechanization, we have broken the Malthusian curse by transitioning from subsistence agriculture, where most of the population is engaged in laboring to provide food, to today, where a single family can manage hundreds of acres. Qatar, a country with less than 2% arable land, became essentially self-sufficient in half a decade. Unfortunately, modern farming made food supply dependent on a complex supply system, requiring the cooperation of many highly concentrated pools of expertise, energy, and transportation logistics. It matters little to the hapless victims of a flood in Indonesia that the US is wasting roughly 40% of its food consumption, and getting sick from overeating at that. It does not take long to die, or for children to suffer from stunted development, when food supply is disrupted. It does not have to happen in the entire world, just the area where you live and a week will be enough to disrupt social order.

> **Ignore what you can't act on.** During an interview with the BBC, Lord Gladstone, then retired, was asked what he thought of the problem in the Middle East, to which he quipped: "there's no problem in the Middle East". After a dramatic pause and gasps from the audience, he continued: "A problem is something that has a solution". Don't worry about what you can't act on.

**Asteroids, earthquakes, volcanoes, hurricanes, and locusts.** Finally, there are acts of God. Earthquakes and volcanoes can strike quickly. Most strike unpredictably.

Most disaster-prone areas have building standards in place to protect from the likeliest catastrophe. It is difficult to prepare beyond that, and harder still to assess probability. Therefore, we generally disregard them and simply consider them as part of the background probability of being hit by anything.

**Cycles**

When dealing with complex systems, it is natural to seek events and trends from the past in order to predict the future. We begin with a model of causes and catalysts for epochs to transition. Models, by their nature, are gross simplifications. Simplification is done in the name of feasibility, and, if the models are to be consumed by humans, so that they fit in our brains. Rare is the successful macro investor. On the other hand, many have been trapped and lost life and treasure for failing to recognize the right time to decamp. We list a few cycle theories, approximately sorted by time horizon, for your consideration. This is by no means exhaustive. Almost all of them point to exceptionally turbulent times ahead. It could be due to a cognitive bias: those who dedicate themselves to the study of history may unconsciously desire for the Big Finale to happen, if only out of curiosity. It also sells more copies of your book that way.

**The Little Ice Age.** Believe it or not, global warming started before acid rain in the 1970s. From approximately 1400 A. D. to 1800 A. D., the climate was unusually cooler. Humanity was very dependent on agriculture, and it was a miserable time. Contrast that with the period from

## 2.2. BAD THINGS HAPPEN

800 B. C. to 500 B. C., when warmer climates prevailed. We ended human sacrifice, stumbled upon democracy, and made great strides in philosophy. In the coming century, desertification in Africa and other places will cause large movements of population and change the distribution of prosperity. Water will play a key role as a natural tailwind or headwind. It will affect river and sea routes as well.

**Price revolutions.** In the "The Great Wave", David Hackett Fisher identifies three price revolutions in Western Europe since the medieval times. They all end up in great turmoil and often a complete reset of the established order. The period of turmoil can last for two centuries. The first featured the plague and the Hundred Years war War, preceding the Renaissance. The second saw the Thirty Years War, famines, the downfall of the Dutch empire, and led to the Enlightenment. The third wave witnessed the fall of the Habsburgs and Ottoman empires; the Industrial Revolution ensued. The next price revolution is about to begin. It's not clear that his model is accurate, but one should bear in mind that periods of stagnation and generally diminished prospects for the whole population can extend for centuries. The experience of high inflation, social disorder, and a long bout of misery is repeated in China, India, and Persia.

**Principles and the cycles of empires.** Ray Dalio, in "Principles", juxtaposes two cycles: a ten-year business cycle against a backdrop of an empire-long cycle. For the latter, he identifies observable factors and a causal chain of events that lead to the rise and fall of empires. As we learn from "Thucydides' Trap" by Graham Allison, a change in world leadership does not usually happen peacefully. Dalio reckons that we are approaching a transition point. His metrics show that American leadership has been deteriorating for some time. It is not as clear to me that China is on the brink on surpassing the United States quickly and decisively as many people believe. Its army, without blue water navy, is untested and is unlikely to have the ability to project force globally in the next decade. Additionally, China's currency does not have an offshore Euro-dollar equivalent, making it unsuitable for widespread use as a reserve, debt denomination, etc. On the other hand, there is a significant possibility that America could blunder and fall precipitously. There is a greater possibility that the chasm of perception between Chinese and American views will lead to tragically silly, avoidable escalations of conflict. There is also a likely bifurcation of systems, similar to a Cold War, which at least halves the trading opportunities.

**Fourth Turning.** A somewhat simplified version of Dalio's world, the "Fourth Turning" by Neil Howe looks at demographic cycles. The first generation, pilgrims, is born into penury and works hard. The second generation inherits the ethics of working hard from their parents, and has a first hand experience of childhood in poverty, but enjoys greater prosperity towards the end. The third generation, born into prosperity, works less hard but access to tales of grandparents and parents about hard times being not far away. The fourth generation, born with a silver spoon, often studying arts and humanities, enjoys prosperity, does not understand the origins of prosperity, and squanders it all. And so we get from rags to rags in three generations. It takes about 80 years for the cycle to play about, and we're in the fourth generation, in case it wasn't clear.

## 2.2. BAD THINGS HAPPEN

**Kondratiev cycle.** Again, a special case of Dalio, the Kondratiev cycle is a 50-year cycle. Instead of demographics, it looks at technology as a driver of changes. It is not clear that the theory can be extrapolated into the future. Over time, however, many economists have made changes and adjustments and it has been a good macro core on which to attach different theories.

**Country-level cycles.** The cycles of rise and decay play out in the context of the broader world, but also within each individual country. Capital controls, expropriation, taxation in your financial home may affect you more than the annexation of Taiwan.

**Business cycles, commodities.** There is a roughly ten-year business cycle of boom and bust, studied by Austrian economist Joseph Schumpeter among others. It's not exactly clear why it tends to occur over a decade. Sometimes it's longer or shorter, and many a times it's blurred by monetary policy. Commodities, and energy in particular, follow ups and downs in demand. Energy infrastructure is costly and slow to upgrade: just as an example, there are 200 million cars in the US, and we sell around 5-10 million each year, so replacing the fleet could take 20 years. That's the typical time it takes for an energy transition.

All in all, you can see that there are forces at play on different scales, ranging from several centuries to several years. If you read recent books, you will be forgiven to believe that all will converge in a massive transformation next year. While this is probably not the case, a generational shift and a large transformation could happen in our 50 years horizon. Empires fall rarely, but when they do, they fall fairly swiftly, in the span of a couple of decades.

### 2.2.2 Some vignettes

Let's take some arbitrary examples to illustrate the various types of events that can occur. In relation to each of these instances, it is essential to contemplate the likely frequency of their occurrence, the effect they may have on your situation and your ability to minimize their impact.

In many cases, you will see that it's the transition that hurts the most.

**476 A. D.** The fall of the Roman empire in the fifth century A. D. marks the beginning of the Middle Ages. This was not a happy time. The population of Rome dwindled from half a million to tens of thousands. The Romans provided vital infrastructure in the empire. Plumbing, irrigation, road networks (such as they were), and sea routes for the transportation of goods and commerce essentially vanished for a thousand years. It's a fantasy to believe that humanity cannot regress in critical technology. Irrigation is paramount to agriculture, which dominated life expectancy and the economy, yet we lost the know-how. We also lost the art of making concrete for a thousand years. It's useful stuff. Today, we produce 4 billion tons of concrete annually, or about half a ton per capita, each and every year. We could lose the ability to go to the moon, have satellite communications, nuclear power, and high-performance chips quite easily. Yet 476 A. D. was not 1453. Those who predicted the fall of the Eastern Roman Empire, the weaker branch, would also have had to wait for a millennium for their predictions to come true.

## 2.2. BAD THINGS HAPPEN

**A year without summer.** In 1883, the Krakatoa (or Krakatau) volcano in Indonesia erupted spectacularly. A sound was heard over 10% of the Earth's area, reaching Perth in Australia, 3000 km away. The blast killed 36,000 people, and reach over 25 miles in the sky. The volcano discharged 21 cubic km over 800,000 sq km. The sky darkened with ashes, and for that year, there was no summer. Global temperatures cooled by 0.4 C to 1.2 C. The tsunami that spread waves that were 46m to 150m high. The Dutch were the most impacted, but by then the economic leadership had been passed on to the British. The impact on the stock market and inflation are significant, but not catastrophic:

| Year | Stock Index | Price Index |
|---|---|---|
| 1880 | 32.99 | 76.21 |
| 1881 | 32.65 | 77.87 |
| 1882 | 33.42 | 78.53 |
| **1883** | 29.48 | 78.91 |
| 1884 | 27.60 | 81.33 |
| 1885 | 27.60 | 83.32 |
| 1886 | 27.35 | 83.35 |
| 1887 | 27.45 | 85.49 |
| 1888 | 26.83 | 86.83 |
| 1889 | 28.59 | 87.91 |
| 1890 | 32.13 | 90.71 |

In 1815, the Tambora (also in present day Indonesia) erupted with more emissions, and again did not cause the end of the world. Economically, I don't worry about a volcanic eruption, earthquake, asteroid, or even a nuclear accident in a minor city.

**Black death.** The bubonic plague was a rodent disease. Diseases have to minimize mortality among their hosts so as to maximize their chances of survival and transmission. Rodents thrive particularly well in urban human settlements, but can live in other places. Humans are just unfortunate collateral damage. The plague had recurring outbreaks spreading over centuries, because the strain survived in mountain and forest habitats. We refer to Norman Cantor's "In the Wake of the Plague" for a full treatment. Notably, because the disease was blind to wealth, education, and gender, it had a leveling effect on socio-economic disparity. Quick successions meant multiple payments of inheritance taxes (feudal relief), decreasing generational wealth. Women would find themselves the last remaining survivors inheriting wealth. In the 14th century, famines amplified the misery. When times are hard, people turn to blame minorities, and some galvanize the anger of the crowd on their enemies. Jews were tortured to confess to poisoning wealth and covertly spreading the disease. Witch hunts were utilized as a means to discourage women from assembly and to suppress their power. It's likely that 40% of the population perished (including from famines).

**China.** If you study history, you must study China. She had the largest GDP 18 out of the last 20 centuries, according to Kissinger. China was the home of 20% of the world's population. Helpfully, unlike the Roman Empire, she did not expand her territory to far and distant lands. When foreign barbarians (Manchus and Mongols) ruled, they were wise enough to avail themselves of the local administration. At times, the power was split in two to six kingdoms, but, by and large, after Emperor Qin unified the country around 221 B.C., China can be regarded

## 2.2. BAD THINGS HAPPEN

as a single country. We have a long history with 55 dynasties, 355 emperors. Each emperor reigned for 11 years on average, and a median of 6 years, roughly in line with the Roman Empire. When studying ancient history, we don't have precise economic series. We use population is a proxy for economic success. The length of reign gives an approximate sense of political stability. Here, we show the distribution of length of reigns of Chinese Emperors. Many would hold the crown for less than a year, and two were at the helm for 60-ish years.

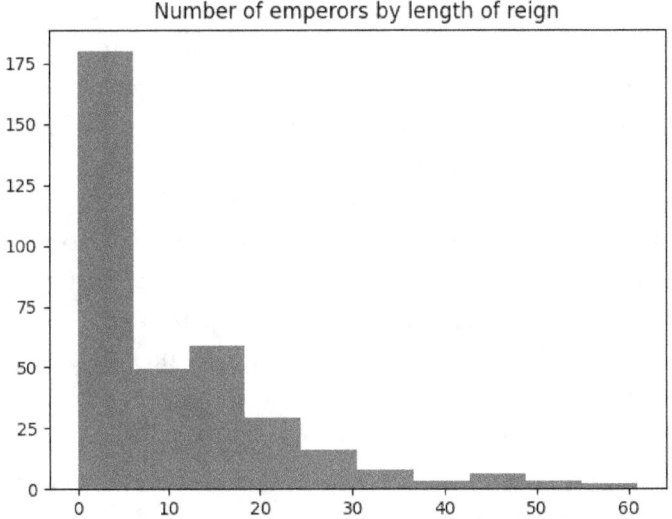

Since the Qin dynasty, over the next 2500 years, there have been only a handful of episodes where the population declined by double digits.

|  | Year(s) | Pop change |
| --- | --- | --- |
| Three Kingdoms | 200-300 | -53% |
| An Lushan rebellion | 755 | -44% |
| Mongol invasion | 1280 | -46% |
| Ming transition, Black death | 1351-1368 | -46%* |
| Qing transition | 1650 | -28% |

Now, the Mongols (Yuan Dynasty) did engage in territorial expansion, so the -46% population decline in the Empire after their rule is simply that the Empire shed its colonies: only about 13 million people died from the Black Death out of about 80 million. All numbers are very, very rough estimates. Speaking of the Mongols, they ushered a rule of strong law, stability and peace, but the transition was anything but peaceful. It's one of the largest mass killings in history, wiping out 11% of total world population, about 50 million in Asia. It is hard to pin down the exact cause for the population declines. Failed crops, poor administration create famines, famines create wars, and vice-versa. Regardless, civil wars appeared to be the deadliest reason for relative population decline. Not pandemics, foreign invasion, earthquakes, crop failures. No, it was squabble at the top, every half a millennia or so, that cut the population in half.

**Substitution effects.** During hyper-inflation, all bets are off. We have economic series measuring baskets of goods throughout the period, but they can be meaningless. In "When Money Dies", Adam Ferguson describes how a well-to-do lady sells her piano for a week of food supplies. Costantino Bresciani-Turroni, in "Economics of Inflation", reports how people turned to eating dog and horse meat during the episode.

## 2.2. BAD THINGS HAPPEN

| Quarter | Animal | Consumption |
|---------|--------|-------------|
| 1921Q1  | Pig    | 1.4M        |
| 1921Q1  | Horse  | 31k         |
| 1921Q3  | Pig    | 1.1M        |
| 1921Q3  | Horse  | 48k         |
| 1921Q3  | Dog    | 1,090       |
| 1922Q3  | Dog    | 3,678       |
| 1923Q3  | Dog    | 6,430       |
| 1924Q3  | Dog    | 841         |

We often look at statistics, but they don't always tell the full story of what happens in reality.

**Great Britain.** Thanks to the quality of its civil servants, Great Britain, as it was then called, has the longevity and documentary statistics for economic historians to analyze. Here, we focus on stock market prices. The Bank of England released a stock market index from different series spanning roughly 300 years. Note that the series don't include dividends, which were made in kind, at a rate of perhaps 5%. The series until 1845 are dominated by two companies: the East India Company and the South Sea Company. We collect the average price over 20 year periods. We will crudely simplify the long and rich history of these three centuries with a highly reductive summary. Britain ran an extractive rule in India. The Industrial Revolution in the realm started around 1760 until 1840. In 1914, the British Empire comprised more than 400 million people or a quarter of the world population. It participated in the two world wars that shattered the old continent. If it wasn't clear by 1956 when it lost the Suez canal, then certainly the debacle of the Falklands in 1982 made it plain that the United Kingdom was no longer the power that it once was. Let's look at stock market prices, in nominal terms and real terms.

| Year | | Nominal | Real |
| Start | End | stock price | stock price |
| --- | --- | --- | --- |
| 1710 | 1730 | 2.30 | 1.78 |
| 1730 | 1750 | 2.75 | 1.81 |
| 1750 | 1770 | 2.79 | 2.17 |
| 1770 | 1790 | 2.70 | 2.06 |
| 1790 | 1810 | 3.33 | 2.32 |
| 1810 | 1830 | 3.68 | 2.55 |
| 1830 | 1850 | 6.72 | 4.11 |
| 1850 | 1870 | 18.79 | 10.16 |
| 1870 | 1890 | 31.55 | 13.69 |
| 1890 | 1910 | 39.38 | 13.13 |
| 1910 | 1930 | 41.88 | 13.08 |
| 1930 | 1950 | 38.58 | 9.93 |
| 1950 | 1970 | 81.24 | 14.46 |
| 1970 | 1990 | 372.28 | 34.87 |
| 1990 | 2010 | 2168.18 | 129.18 |

We have been blessed with a high level of prosperity of late but in fact there are many 40-year periods where stock market returns have been nil or negative in real terms. From the second industrial revolution (think rail, cars, planes, and electricity) from 1870 to 1970 (just after the war), we would have had essentially zero returns in that century in real terms. One pound invested in stock market during the greatest technology boom in history would have just retained its purchasing power. We understand that improvements in lifespan, sanitation, etc make the average life in 1870 (anesthesia was a new thing then) look brutish and short compared to 1970, but they do occur at

## 2.2. BAD THINGS HAPPEN

a pace which is easy to get used to. This is one third of the 3 centuries of data and twice our time horizon. So, there are secular epochs where we cannot rely solely on the stock market.

**Lambert function.** The Lambert $W$ function is the solution of a transcendental equation, that is, an equation mixing a variable in its exponential and natural forms. They occur naturally in differential equations, and places where you mix product and sum, such as compounding growth (product) of a portfolio (sum). As a scientist, I recognized that it could be useful one day and have been looking for an opportunity to use it for the last quarter of a century, without success. Warren Buffett watched silver prices for 40 years before he committed less than 2% of Berkshire's portfolio to it. You have to keep your eyes open and be ready to act quickly for something that may never happen. That requires patience.

### 2.2.3 Consequences

**When goods stop crossing borders, armies do.** Louis Bastiat, the French libertarian, author of The Law, stated that nations would exchange bullets when they finished exchanging goods. Commerce provides a vested interest to keep a relationship going, and it's much more productive than wars. Look for signs of cooling trade.

**Defenestration.** It is said that vocabulary reflects the values of a culture. Arabic has numerous words for horses to distinguish between fine differences. Reviving a dormant word in Middle French, and predating a certain Russian leader, whose name may resemble a Quebec dish of fries and cheese, by several centuries, Prague popularized the habit of throwing people out of a window, preferably from a great height, and of the opposing religious creed or high in the social ladder. Medieval Europe boasts a rich tradition of purges.

So, we know that big stuff can happen. Picture one situation. Let's say a volcano erupted, leaving the earth under an ashen sky for a decade. Health issues, failing crops, cooling temperatures ensue. Famines break out in some parts of the world. Countries start stockpiling goods and tensions rise, reducing commerce among nations. Productivity declines, and lower standards of living are needed. Instability in the stock market is the norm. Generations lose their life savings through inflation and stock market losses, while a handful of individuals, gamblers and cheaters, concentrate wealth and flaunt it. Social unrest is boiling up. The government, in von Mises' phrase, "the social apparatus of coercion and compulsion", tilts from police and protection of property, to pitchforks and mob violence. Country borders are redrawn with the sword, unleashing seizure of land and lives across weaker nations. So what?

You're minding your own business, retired at home. Still, there are many ways these large events can affect you.

## 2.2. BAD THINGS HAPPEN 47

**Life in danger.** The most basic property you have to secure is your own life. You have to make arrangements to live in a community that you trust, away from access to large mobs. Wars strike large centers of population first. Cities are places where specialization occurs and the supply chain is most fragile.

**Inability to obtain essential life necessities.** Supply chains may be disrupted, and power may be cut. You may have to relocate to a shelter where you cannot store goods and otherwise valuable items securely. Water, food, life-saving medicine, shelter are the next items to secure.

**Inability to procure basic goods.** Some goods are required for livelihood. Light bulbs. Perhaps a computer. Or a refrigerator. If you have a car or own a home, maintenance items should be secured. Some stockpiling should be relatively easy.

**Inability to procure basic services.** You cannot perform all maintenance yourself, especially as you age. Basic services, such as medical care, plumbing, and electrical work, all rely on labor that, in times of turmoil, tend to be highly inflated, dishonest and otherwise unreliable.

**Breakdown of trust.** In survival mode, it's everyone for himself and God for us all. You cannot rely on commercial transactions to be properly enforced. Theft and extortion can be expected. If you're the kind of person who gets cheated at the car dealer, expect this to happen everywhere.

**Expropriation.** Populist governments are a slightly more orderly version of pitchforks. They will abrogate property rights as they please. It is hard to predict which areas will be targeted. Providers of essential goods and services and land owners are typical targets. For convenience, the middle class is targeted because it has wealth, follows the law, and lacks the political connections to protect itself. In case of invasions or local breakdown of property rules, physical items and bank accounts are likely to be seized. With biometrics and digital money, it is becoming near impossible to move wealth across jurisdictions.

**Taxes.** Taxes are a more gradual form of expropriation. Up until World War II, government spending was below 20% of GDP. Then, it gradually crept up to 40%. To maintain your purchasing power, your stocks and bonds have to earn a return equal to the inflation, plus tax – effectively a form of wealth tax. We refer to Charles Adams' "For Good and Evil" for a discussion on morality and maximum rates of extraction that elicit a Fight, Flight or Fraud response.

**Income tax after inflation is a wealth tax.** Let's imagine you save one dollar and live 36 years into retirement. Put the case, further, that inflation averaged 2% annualized during that period. You had a wealth-preservation scheme that preserved the purchasing power of that dollar exactly. Therefore, by the rule of 72, you would have two dollars at the end of your retirement. Your capital gain would have been one (future) dollar. If your tax rate is 25%, you would have to pay 12.5% just to preserve your wealth. An inflation rate of 3%-5% and a 30% capital gains tax should be expected, so your last dollars should be discounted by about 23%.

**Inflation, extreme inflation.** Inflation is an insidious tax. Government overspends. Federal Reserve monetizes the debt (allows credit growth to mop up new debt).

## 2.2. BAD THINGS HAPPEN

Purchasing power of dollar decreases. Government blames profiteers and speculators for pain. Government creates spending programs to ease the pain, lowering efficiency and raising costs in targeted areas. Rinse, repeat. Moderate inflation is easier to deal with. Some assets, such as enterprises dealing with health and food, gold, are expected to offset inflation (modulo taxes). Extreme inflation, in the style of pre-war Germany or Zimbabwe, result in the destruction of the fabric of society. It only takes a year or two. In that event, leaving the country altogether to wait it out might be the best option. Debt is forgiven.

**Capital controls.** In the 1964 movie, James Bond, Her Majesty's top spy is on a mission to thwart a villain. The worst kind, naturally. A nuclear terrorist, perhaps? A drug lord, you fancy? A communist? A human trafficking overlord, surely? The leader of a new sect? No, Auric Goldfinger is in the business of moving gold covertly out of the United Kingdom. The British pound was backed by gold, so moving gold meant leaking the backing of pounds out of the country, evading capital controls. Unless you want to be chased by spies, I suggest you comply with government restrictions on moving money outside the country. Interestingly, since Nixon's demonetization of gold, the yellow metal is no longer considered money. Instead, it's categorized as jewelry or a commodity. Diamonds were used by Jews during World War II, but illiquid markets at high denominations and non-fungibility meant that a lot of wealth was lost in the process. Asset swaps, where money inside the country is used to offset a liability abroad, are hard to find when money is trying to flee. The best is to move wealth as money before capital controls are enforced.

**Denial of financial services.** In Canada, covid-19 vaccine protesters had their bank accounts frozen by the government. Doing commerce with, or investing in an enterprise overseas might get you blacklisted. If you have a business, the illiquidity might just destroy the venture. The problem is that a small minority of people might get targeted, not enough to trigger widespread popular support. You can have the law, even the Constitution on your side, but that won't help a temporary lock out. These sanctions could happen during relatively innocuous times and a hard to prepare against. Geographical diversification might not help. It's possible to have some gold buried in your backyard but impractical to keep all your net worth outside of the banking system at all times. If you want to avoid trouble, don't be the tall grass.

**Nowhere to hide - financial repression.** The government loves to spend. The United States is the most powerful nation on Earth, and also the biggest debtor. It is in the interest of debtors to find covert ways to seek forgiveness. If interest rates obtained by creditors do not compensate for inflation, then the debt burden is slowly vanishing. It creates a situation where savings must find riskier ways to seek returns – corporate debt and riskier investments.

**Targeted repression: rent controls, etc.** The way inflation works is that the Federal Reserves loosens the reins on the creation of - credit. The banks are then more willing to lend to businesses and aspiring home owners. Businesses then buy goods and more homes are bought. Those who receive the money then spend it. As observed by Richard Cantillon, money slowly diffuses from bank credit

## 2.2. BAD THINGS HAPPEN 51

to all parts of the economy through a process called transmission. It is a mystery at what speed and to which sectors the money flows. For moral or economic reasons, the interventionist government, typically of a populist bend, will attempt to control this diffusion by limiting, by law, certain price increases. Historically, rent controls have been put in place. Windfall taxes could occur at the most profitable and visible parts of the economy. They are usually applied immediately or retroactively and leave no time to prepare.

**Returning to lower prosperity and productivity for an extended period.** During times of lower prosperity, everyone is less happy, for good reason. The stock market may experience lackluster returns and higher risk for decades. It should be a period of deflation that benefit creditors (people with savings) and property owners, but it is likely that the government and the Federal Reserve will implement a regime of financial repression aimed at suppressing the rentier class.

**Extreme volatility.** In many situations, dire as they may seem, it is possible to devise a strategy that will counter the ill effects of a certain kind. Ownership in agriculture, for instance, can help alleviate food inflation. However, it is extreme uncertainty and volatility that are hard to guard against. They also tend to generate civil unrest and destabilize order. So, in that case, staying put in the bunker with your gold might work well to wait it out for a year.

**Permanent regression in technology.** As we have seen, we have witnessed the loss of know-how for certain technologies over extended periods of time. Technology plays a significant role in various aspects of our lives, ranging from the internet and electricity to transport, irrigation, agriculture, and more. We often overlook the numerous amenities that we take for granted. Some business higher up in the chain may face extinction.

**Permanent regression in profitability, and higher risk.** We are living in an unprecedented period of growth and progress. It will end or suffer some interruption at some point. Then, profitability of enterprises will settle at a lower level. Interest rates will be nominally higher to compensate for higher default rates. Stock market returns will be lower. Productivity gains will be lower. In general, the need for ready money today to fund future growth will diminish, leaving gains from the employ of capital permanently lower for all asset classes.

**Unanticipated liability.** You may feel obligated to intervene with all your might and resources if a family member or close friend, is in a sudden need of money. This could be the death of the bread-winner. If that's a potential issue, make sure everyone has a life insurance. You may have to go back to work.

**Lawsuits.** Suing for damages is a profitable national sport in the United States. You should house major assets under a Limited Liability Company, or a trust, or a combination of thoseof. Trust law is changing and new protections have become available in the last decade. It is possible to protect asssets from lawsuits, and in some cases from taxation as well.

**Built-in inflation.** Satoshi Nakamoto, the elusive creator of bitcoin, holds 5% of all bitcoins, or $60 billion at the current price in

## 2.2. BAD THINGS HAPPEN 53

2024. His portfolio is largely dormant. There is a point where it might be worth for a state actor to build a specialized facility to crack his keys. Or perhaps more cheaply, coerce the five key bitcoin developers to introduce a subtle flaw in the code.

**Encryption.** The strength of encryption is typically designed to be sufficiently robust for the next 50 years of computing advances. So far, advances in algorithms can be expected to halve this, and with quantum computing, I would fully expect any communications through the web (https), if stored, to be fully crackable with very modest power within the next couple of decades. That lowers the bar from state actors to merely organized crime. Storage and patience are expensive so they have to be selective. Any encryption at rest (storage) should select a prohibitively high encryption grade (note that cracking difficulty is exponentional in the length of key, whereas normal usage is simply linear). You cannot choose what websites use, and it tends to be weak and insecure. The best defense is to remain under the radar and hope that both criminals and governments will deem your communications unworthy of their interest. Hopefully, quantum communications will be introduced in the meanwhile, which make passive snooping impossible.

Some disruptions may be brief, while others may last indefinitely. For example, you can gather enough food to sustain yourself for a couple of months. But if you anticipate that supplies will be prohibitively expensive for years on end, then consider owning farmland in a secure area close to your residence.

You may choose to buy a farm and build property somewhere other than your primary residence. It is cheaper and you may still enjoy the amenities of city living. However, understand that moving there is an extra step and you may be the proverbial boiled frog. If you were in Ukraine in February 2022, healthy male of fighting age, within a week the unimaginable happened and it was too late to leave the country. Within a week, covid-19 measures effectively shut down all flights for extended periods. Australians were denied the right to return to their own country. Don't take mobility for granted.

### 2.2.4 Thriving

We have established that bad things can happen with real consequences to our retirement. There is an uncommon risk to our assets and life that require preparation that it outside of the norm of rearranging liquid wealth amongst asset classes.

First, we would like to withstand the initial onslaught of the disaster. Second, we wish to adapt and thrive in the new environment. Nassim Taleb introduced the concept of anti-fragility: the further things go south, the better we do.

In all cases, those preparations will cost money and resources. It is up to you to decide how much you would like to allocate to an event that will probably happen only once in your retirement.

## 2.2. BAD THINGS HAPPEN

**Live**

During crises, you have to go back to basics. It's not about projecting the 5-year impact on profits of a logo change in Apple. Rather, it is about securing your daily necessities about you and preserving your wealth. Your homes, financial and physical, are under attack.

**Jurisdiction.** Your financial home should be in a safe place. Switzerland is a generally non-aligned country (formerly called Third World), known for its stability and adherence to the rule of law. Unfortunately, due to abuse, it has become a target for the United States, and it has since lost many of the protections it once afforded. Singapore has the right culture and know-how, where your assets are safe and managed professionally, but it is a small island that relies on military protection from the United States. The Strait is a strategic choke point from the Middle East to China, which is why, thanks to its stable property respecting government, it is the home of important infrastructure such as refineries. It could also be the Suez Canal of Asia that, when invaded, might show the true vulnerability of the United States. The Cook Islands, best known for divorce protection, offer superior asset protection. They comply with international money-laundering and anti-terrorism laws, which allows them some reprieve. The United States could decide one day that Russia is a terrorist state and all assets should be forfeited. It is best to live close to your financial assets, *ceteris paribus*. It's also good to diversify your brokerage accounts, in general.

**Offshore finance for non-aligned citizens.** If you hail from an non-aligned country, the USA is the biggest offshore finance hub. The landscape changes frequently, so it's best to consult a specialist. Trusts and bank accounts in Nevada, Wyoming, and Delaware are most popular today. They are not subject to either US FATCA or European CRS reporting (for non US persons).

**Passports.** In a bifurcated world, to simplify, USA vs China, you will have to think about your passport strategy. Non-aligned countries look benign to either block and should enjoy the benefits of neutrality. Holding a passport could be a liability. Not a century ago, the US "interned" more than 100 thousand people of Japanese descent, most of them American citizens. A passport is not a guarantee of protection or restriction-free travel, but in most cases it will work.

**When to move.** Obviously, don't wait until it's too late. You can read about the atrocities experienced by boat people fleeing from Vietnam or North Korea (see "Nothing To Envy" by Barbara Demick). The main obstacle is usually lack of preparation. People postpone jumping into the unknown. Have a plan for moving liquid assets and other possessions, family, at the ready. People in Ukraine in 2022 were given less than two weeks warning. Conscription in Russia gave people no advance warning. If you don't have a plan, it's likely that you will postpone until it's too late. It's a good idea to live somewhere for, say, a month or so to try out retirement, and to see how you cope with packing your bags and living in a foreign environment.

**Community.** When basic trust breaks down, supply chains are disrupted, and you revert to barter, different rules apply. At this stage, you will be well served to have established good relationships within your local community. People help friends in times of need and turn against

## 2.2. BAD THINGS HAPPEN

strangers or minorities, at the point of a gun.

**Farm and bunker.** A small farm, enough for your own needs (say 5 or 6 acres), will give you the most resilience. You don't need a total breakdown of society for a farm to be useful. High inflation will do. A big resilient farm is a full-time job, so aim small. Living in a bunker could protect your valuable possessions and your life from humans and weather alike. If you have one, it's a good place to store physical gold in small denominations. You need about 1 kg per person at a minimum.

**Non-urban area.** When picking a place to weather a storm, a non-urban area tends to be better. Looting happens in high density areas. Densely populated areas are targets for bombing. They also rely on more complex infrastructure, for electricity (elevators enabled high rises in the 1930s), water treatment, etc. It is cheaper and easier to have a farm in a less populated area, with more space and natural resources for everyone.

**Access to basic supplies and services.** On the other hand, unless you are fully sufficient, you don't want to live too far out. You may need food and water supplies, access to basic services for maintenance and repair. Hospitals are critical pieces of infrastructure which are usually not the target of bombing, and receive immediate attention if damaged. If you live near a hospital, you will have easy access to medical care, and, likely electricity and water.

### Prosper

Aside from rearranging your financial assets, are there any other ways to benefit from times of turbulence? Who are the types of individuals that not only survive but thrive in a tough environment?

**Thugs.** When the government no longer holds the monopoly of violence, those who can appropriate local parcels enjoy the benefits of the state – taxation. Mafia organizations and oligarchs do well. Choosing this lifestyle is incongruent with the other goals of your retirement: living a healthy, long life and living a life of meaning. Nonetheless, you will have to accommodate for new arrangements.

**Liars and thieves.** When law enforcement fades, those who would otherwise get punished can flourish unabated. They establish a new norm of dishonesty and mistrust which percolates through the entire society.

**Farmers and handymen.** Providers of basic necessities and services should thrive. Nurses and healthcare providers will be in high demand, especially if violence escalates. Owning a tractor or any other piece of equipment could be profitable. We suggest you play in this area.

**Mid-rank administration.** For 125 generations, the Japanese Imperial clan has seen it all, including an interruption of two and a half centuries in its rule, called the Edo period or shogunate. After that, the monarchy was restored in what was called the Meiji restoration. Yet, in 1945, when General MacArthur took over the reorganization of the country, this old institution was almost abolished. Instead, MacArthur decided to preserve the order. It is often wise not to rock the boat if you are interested in rebuilding a more stable country. The Zaibatsu (literally money clans) are large commercial vertically integrated conglomerates. There were four main ones after the war: two were founded during the Edo period and two during the Meiji restoration. There was a half-hearted attempt to dissolve these structures but they survived, and thrived. The Zaibatsu were family-owned, and while they had to restructure their ownership, by and large, they did quite well. If you are an essential part of the industrial base, ownership may change via nationalization. The management and administration has a better chance to survive.

## 2.3 Classical financial planning

Now that we have looked at the once-in-a-lifetime events, let's think about the rest. There are rough seas, but not tsunamis. Most of retirement literature focuses on the question of how much you should save and how should you allocate your portfolio during retirement. Simple rules are given. They are, by and large, reasonable. Our objective here is to understand the assumptions and potential pitfalls.

### 2.3.1 Framework

We refer the reader to the excellent books of Wade Pfau for detailed and clear explanations on the topic. Financial retirement advice follows the rough outline:

1. Estimate how much you are going to need in retirement.

2. Find an optimal portfolio allocation.

3. Estimate how long your savings can stretch.

This is reasonable enough at first blush, especially for the rigor that is demanded of academic study. It will work fairly well for short retirement durations of a couple of decades. Assumptions are reasonable for academia, but sometimes fall short of realistic expectations. For instance, in studying the withdrawal rate, the notion of "failure", that is, running out of money, is defined and odds of, say, 5% (one in twenty chance) are typical. If you have the choice to delay retirement, it's not a rate that you'll be comfortable with, and, at least, you will look for mitigation strategies.

Another case in point, the perspective on long-term care is to cover the cost of medical and living expenses in a managed facility. This is reasonable from a financial standpoint. However, in reality, money is merely the beginning. With mental and physical capacities waning with old age, trust becomes a crucial factor. No one will check that the caregiver is doing their job, no one has the ability to complain. At an advanced age, one is at the mercy of the caregiver. Often, family members are the only available trusted option. It can take decades to groom a relationship with a surviving person. Finance is a quantifiable, controllable part of the equation and classical financial planning does a reasonable job.

To be clear, we take a different approach:

1. We do not plan precisely for average spend. We care about the fat tail of spending shocks and capital preservation.

2. As explained later, we will use a pre-dominantly stock portfolio with a catastrophe edge.

## 2.3. CLASSICAL FINANCIAL PLANNING

3. While we do accept that there is a possibility of failure despite our best preparations, we do not estimate failure probabilities. We strive to continually minimize the possibility of failure throughout retirement, by minimizing dependencies (see the chapter on **Purpose**, and the concept of unconditioned happiness).

This is not to say that classical financial planning is irrelevant. But, by and large, a rough back-of-the-envelope calculation is all we need. It's impossible to be precise (a quality prized by academic above correctness and common sense), instead we focus on the accuracy and confidence of the estimate. For instance, in classical financial retirement planning, we aim to die with fully depleted resources, no more, no less. In practice, however, the desirability is highly asymmetric, and we would err on the side of dying with a comfortable cushion rather than risking any probability of facing destitution. With that in mind, let's see what we can plan.

### 2.3.2 Spend in retirement

First, we need to determine what cash flow we need. It's important to understand the difference between cash flow and total net worth. In a typical case, we don't have all of the money we need upfront. We'll need to rely on cash flow generated from investments. The total net worth is a just tool for generating income, not money that we spend directly. It's not a piggy bank from which we are withdrawing little by little. If you assume a 3.3% income from investments, then each dollar of annual cash flow necessitates approximately $30 dollars in net worth to back it up.

That $10 monthly magazine subscription is equivalent to a $3600 one-time splurge on your bucket list cruise trip. They are both denominated in dollars but there's a 30x difference.

Moreover, both spend and income are subject to variations that are not strictly under your control. The stock market may go down for a couple of years, and it's not worth the frictional costs of downgrading your living quarters for a few years. During that time, your spend will exceed your average projected spend. Moreover, you might find that it is difficult to make lifestyle adjustments. Lifestyle is a part of our identity, and powerful habits are hard to give up. Don't overestimate your ability to adjust to a lower spending rate.

Variations in spending are not entirely unpredictable. We refer to Wade Pfau's book for the different kinds of persona that can serve as templates to map your spending profile over the years. Most tend to follow a smile curve, where spending decreases when we reach middle age and increases again, and most steeply in old age when long-term care is required. We generally split in three phases: go-go years, slow-go years, and no-go years. In youthful years, you might pursue expensive hobbies, travel around the world, and accumulate expensive toys. When passions subside, you settle into a simpler lifestyle, perhaps developing relationships with family and friends, and spend less than before. In your sunset years, you are unable to fix the house yourself, cook, care for yourself, and may require medical interventions. A dedicated care-taker might increase your cost of living.

Inflation is commonly understood as a broad measure of

## 2.3. CLASSICAL FINANCIAL PLANNING

cost of living. The mix of housing, medical costs, insurance, food and entertainment varies from person to person. In times of euphoria, you can expect the commodity curve to lower the cost of common luxury goods. During periods of depressed economic activity, energy will cost more. Rent may increase at double digit rates and stay elevated: it won't affect home owners.

Additionally, some financial planners advocate for estimating spend based on current income. This is a quick and dirty method that may work for individuals with a low savings rate. If you retire early, I suggest you refrain from using this method.

Finally, you should provision some amount for spending shocks. These include medical expenses as a result of an accident or illness, education costs, divorce fees, etc. They are one-time events.

You now have a rough idea of how much money you will need, roughly speaking, as well as the range of adjustments that you can make, should some correction be required. Oddly, in classical financial planning, this phase is typically completely ignored during withdrawal calculation.

### 2.3.3 Withdrawal amount

Now, we come from the other side of the equation. Given your initial net worth when retiring, how much can you expect to be able to withdraw without running out of money? Previously, we looked at how much you *needed*, now we're looking at how much you *can* spend.

First, we will define withdrawal as a percentage of total net worth at any given time. Let's say you have a million dollars and we're looking at a 4% withdrawal rate: you can spend $40,000 per year. Put the case where, through luck or skill, you grow that million dollars to five million dollars, we're now looking at $200,000 per year. It's reasonable to assume that there is a tendency to spend up to the limit that we can. If, on the other hand, your portfolio gets cut in half to $500,000, then it means that you would need to adjust to a lifestyle that is near the poverty line. While this assumption is not realistic, it is convenient.

The most famous rule-of-thumb in retirement planning is the 4% rule. It stipulates that you can spend 4% of your total net worth during retirement and deplete your assets at the end of your life. This is called the Bengen study, and its minor variation by Trinity College in Cambridge arrives at similar results. This excludes the tax drag. It does not use bootstrap re-sampling (uses the observed sequence of returns in the last century). It does not take account of the fact that most investors underperform the broad stock market index by a wide margin. It does not use the smile curve of spend. It does not take income from social security. It does not enforce minimum withdrawal limits on retirement accounts. Despite its many drawbacks, it is a suitable starting point, provided that we understand that it is likely to be optimistic, especially for periods longer than 30 years.

There are a number of superior planners out there. Once you need to re-sample and take into account more realistic assumptions, you will typically need to use a Monte-Carlo simulation. You will also have to input more variables, such as expected tax rate, portfolio composition, and expected inflation rate. It's impossible to know what the

## 2.3. CLASSICAL FINANCIAL PLANNING

future holds for us, so the added precision sometimes comes with diminished accuracy, so it's not always clear that it will yield a better way to forecast. I have been using the simulator provided by Fidelity LLC, the investment house. Its underlying assumptions are opaque and likely a trade secret, so in my mind it's unsuited for life-changing decisions, but it gives a useful estimate for a rough first cut. For your perusal, Internet personality Rob Berger tracks retirement calculators and tools.

We have assumed a 100% US equities portfolio, which is usually too risky for retirement. Oddly again, the withdrawal rate is typically considered independently of the composition of the portfolio.

### 2.3.4 Portfolio allocation

Finally, we need to allocate the portfolio among different asset classes. The main objective is to align with the findings of the two previous studies: to provide money when we need it. The further we look into the future, that larger the uncertainty surrounding the actual portfolio value. Consequently, in the far future, maximizing the probability that we will have enough money boils down to simply maximizing total net worth.

Let us first restrict our study to only two options: a stock market tracker fund and a fixed mix of bonds. Remarkably, there is no definitive answer on how to allocate funds. Mathematically, it all seems so easy. For the purpose of the argument, let us imagine the following returns:

| Year | Portfolio value | Return |
|---|---|---|
| 0 | $100 | - |
| 1 | $80 | -20% |
| 2 | $96 | +20% |
| Average return | | 0% |
| True return (CAGR) | | -2% |

If you put your money in this fund, you would have lost 4% over two years. This evil twin of compounding is called the volatility tax. If you dig yourself into a hole, you'll have to jump higher than the depth of the hole to get back to even. The more pronounced the valleys are, the bigger the tax. Mathematically, the geometric average returns – CAGR, compounded annual growth rate – is guaranteed to be below the arithmetic average returns: you always pay for volatility. It is the Jensen inequality applied to the logarithmic function:

$$\sum_k \log x_k \leq \log \left( \sum_k x_k \right).$$

There is a trade-off between demanding higher returns and reducing volatility. The proportion of bonds in the portfolio is a knob that allows us to dampen returns and volatility, leading to overall higher true returns. If we know what the volatility in the future is, and if we assume stock market returns without fat tails, then it is possible to derive simple analytic solutions for the optimal mix. This is called the Kelly criterion. Markowitz won a Nobel prize for generalizing to multiple securities. It is possible to use more realistic returns with fat tails by using Monte Carlo simulations. Once we are free from the shackles of analytic solutions, we can also enter arbitrary withdrawal rate rules. Still, volatil-

## 2.3. CLASSICAL FINANCIAL PLANNING

ity in the future is unknown and piling up more and more assumptions and uncertain estimates will not make the optimal allocation more accurate. There's a lot of academic work and superstition alike that seek to improve with more complex variants. They are not worth it.

**What we don't know, we just don't know.** John Maynard Keynes was a flamboyant thinker. He wrote: "By uncertain knowledge, I do not mean merely to distinguish what is known for certain from what is only probable. [...] There is no scientific basis to form any calculable probability whatever. We simply do not know."

Unfortunately, while it is very easy to devise the optimal portfolio with knowledge of the future, in reality, the uncertainty surrounding the estimates is so large that we can't decisively tell that one allocation is superior to another, within reason. Therefore, the age-old 60/40% rule (stocks vs. bonds), while not based on solid and sophisticated thinking, is not unreasonable. Neither is the rule that allocates a quarter to each of cash, stocks, commodities, and real estate. The Barbell strategy allocates a small fraction in high risk, extraordinary payoffs, while the majority stays within low-risk. It is very suited to capital preservation for active managers.

If you don't want to spend any time managing your portfolio, following a broadly diversified allocation among asset classes is as good a choice as any. In fact, statistically, active retail investors will overwhelmingly underperform a pure stock index allocation. Most active managers, after fees, will also underperform.

On the topic of matching withdrawal from funds to needs, target funds are also popular, as is the rule that you should hold a percentage of stocks equal to 100 minus your age. This dampens the returns and volatility in your old age, when the advantages of compounding are minimal. You should be aware of sequence risk. A loss early on may force you to liquidate assets to sustain your cash flow, resulting in a permanent loss. Let's say you retire early, with a million dollars. You grow that portfolio with a CAGR of 6% per annum, in inflation-adjusted terms. You have a constant spending rate of $50,000. You live for 50 years. It should all fit, but it may not. Let's imagine that you have returns of 6% every single year, except two: one with a 50% down, followed by a year with 224%. (You have to double your money and make up for slightly twice the 6% return.) You can experience that in your first two years, or in your last two years. Let's look at the difference:

| Year | First | Last |
|---|---|---|
| 0 | $1m | $1m |
| 1 | $450k | $1.01m |
| 2 | $1.008m | $1.02m |
| ... | ... | ... |
| 48 | $3.4m | $3.6m |
| 49 | $3.5m | $1.7m |
| 50 | $3.7m | $3.8m |

Early on, the loss is gut-wrenching. You're down to 9 years of living expenses equivalent savings instead of 20. Closer to the end, the loss is immaterial to your financial needs. But, in overall numbers, the loss in compounding

## 2.3. CLASSICAL FINANCIAL PLANNING

is minuscule. Higher compounding rates will magnify the difference, but, in terms of risk of running out of money, the conclusion is the same. Short-lived down drafts have no impact on your portfolio, so short market panics followed by quick, over-sized monetary and fiscal responses in the style of 2020 don't matter. Long depressions in inflation-adjusted terms in style of 1930s or 1970s can hurt you more if they happen early. When we're talking decades of below-trend returns, then they're a threat no matter what. There's no need to do anything more special early on.

### 2.3.5 Mitigation strategies

What if, despite all your best preparations, you ran out of money? Let's plan for failure. Again, in classical financial planning, this is mostly ignored. You have four options: going to back to work, reducing your spending, living off of someone else's kindness, and, in some cases, dying early. As you age, your choices dwindle.

As a rule, you can achieve maximum resilience by needing less. This is not to say that you can't enjoy the finer life if it presents to you, but you should develop your mind to be able to cut your dependencies if needed. This can be practiced through fasting and living lean months every now and then.

Usually, you would start to implement spending reduction techniques early rather than waiting until you actually run out of money. Similarly, you could build relationships with individuals who would support you in your later years, should the need occur. Financially, they could look like reverse mortgages: you are taken care of until the end, and if there are remaining assets, they go to your caretaker. You could front-load your contribution by paying for someone's education.

## 2.4 Buffer strategy

Classical financial planning works great when you want to get a quick and dirty estimate of where you stand. As the reality of retirement approaches, however, there is a strategy that might give you more confidence.

### 2.4.1 Outline

The goal of the strategy is to provide cash flow when you need it throughout retirement. One way to achieve this is to have an inflation-protected bonds portfolio. However, considering our time frame, this strategy will slowly draw on your reserves until depletion prior to your final demise. Hence, we would like to participate in capital appreciation opportunities with the money we don't use immediately. Unfortunately, these opportunities come at the cost of liquidity: sometimes, it can take years to come to fruition. How do we reconcile a guarantee of having cash now while still employing some in productive ventures?

First, our time scale is half a century, longer than is typical in classical financial planning. We consider the statistical properties of asset prices, which can be unintuitive. With fat tails, you must concern yourself with extraordinary events that can wipe out decades of capital appreciation. They can come swiftly and unexpectedly and can

## 2.4. BUFFER STRATEGY

take decades to repair.

Second, we consider the question of where the income should come from. We look at stocks, fixed income, and gold. Stock ownership is participation in a productive enterprise, sharing risk and profit. Fixed income is renting capital for immediate use. Gold and precious metals preserve capital and gain naturally as society improves productivity.

Third, observing that stocks provide good returns in the long run, we use a cash buffer and dividend stream to withstand a reasonably long bout of lean returns to sustain our cash flow unscathed.

### 2.4.2 It rarely matters greatly

Nassim Taleb, author of The Black Swan, has written at long length about fat tails and the many ways we humans are misled by our intuition. Worse, engineers and scientists, people trained in dealing with statistics and digital signals, often fall prey to the same errors.

**Zero times infinity.** I had lunch with a few fellow scientists at a conference recently. The discussion turned to what the result of zero times infinity was. If you can find two series that approach the operation, but converge to two different results, then the result is undefined. In this case,

$$\lim_{n \to \infty} 0 \cdot n = 0$$

$$\lim_{n \to \infty} \frac{1}{n} \cdot \infty = 0$$

If we think about zero as the probability of an event occurring, and infinity as the payoff (or loss), then we are confused. Does it matter not at all (zero result)? Or does it matter greatly (infinite result)?

Rarely, something comes up that is so important that it negates decades of consistent results. We tend to underestimate its potential impact.

**What you see is not what you get.** It is second nature for us to think about average returns. But what is the average compounded annual return of the US stock market, really? Let's see. We compute the annual return for the following 20 years, adjusted for dividends and inflation:

| Year | CAGR |
|------|--------|
| 1930 | 2.05%  |
| 1940 | 9.70%  |
| 1950 | 10.82% |
| 1960 | 1.82%  |
| 1970 | 4.95%  |
| 1980 | 13.16% |
| 1990 | 5.26%  |
| 2000 | 3.78%  |

Over the period of 1928 to 2023, the annual real return for the stock market was 6.4%. This does not correct for taxes. So, if you had measured the average of different periods for 20 years, you would not have reached a reliable conclusion. You can't make a exact statement about what returns you are supposed to get in the next 20 or 50 years. It's probably above 2% and below 10%. So, here's the first surprising takeaway: the observed average doesn't tell

## 2.4. BUFFER STRATEGY

you much about the true average of the distribution. In technical terms, the empirical mean doesn't approximate the expected value well. Conversely, the expected value is rather meaningless in predicting the next sample empirical mean: even if the real return was truly well estimated at 6%, you can't expect that the average for the next 20 years will be 6%. There's too much variation around the mean. What you don't know, you just don't know: don't make it up, even if it's something as basic as the long-term average return of the stock market.

**Convergence.** All financial historical studies start with the familiar proviso: the past is not guidance for the future. Engineers and lay people alike tend to extrapolate from the past. This is usually a good idea. There are many phenomena in nature that, if observed a handful of times, we can quickly learn to predict. This is based on the assumption of rapid convergence:

1. Applying the central limit theorem states that the average of a distribution will eventually converge to a normal (well-behaved) distribution.

2. Applying the Cramér-Rao lower bound or Student distribution to the estimate, we find that, in practice, about 10 data points are sufficient to approximate parameters extremely well.

3. There is an analog for the central limit theorem which gives the distribution of the minimum expected value, in our case, a Gumbel distribution (as per results from Fisher, Tippett, and Gnedenko).

4. We assume that samples are fairly independent.

5. We assume that the distribution will not change over the observation window (stationarity).

Without going into technical details, all premises of the theorems that we usually use are violated. Whereas it's usually possible to add fudge factors in the form of margin of error, in the case of returns on financial assets, it's simply invalid. We do learn from the past, but very, very slowly, to the point of irrelevance in many cases. We can't expect accurate predictions.

**Your total net worth.** Anyone who's been watching their nest egg nervously every day, knows that, curiously, one's total net worth is not easily measured. One day it will be some amount, and a week later it might have shed 5%. Less than 6 months after I retired, the covid-19 crash happened, and suddenly I was down 15%. Know that, when you retire, you can't measure your total net worth that precisely. Technically, we say that the point estimate is not reliable. Averaging over the last few years will smooth out big moves, if any. For the (downward) moves that have not been seen, you can guesstimate them and leave some padding in your estimate.

**Ergodicity and leverage.** In mathematics, there is a notion of ergodicity. Say there is a beetle in a football field, but that football field has one opening. If the opening is closed, the beetle can roam around for eternity, and will eventually visit every patch of grass on the field. If the opening is opened, then the beetle can escape and that will be the end of it. It's a metaphor for stock market returns. You never want to go totally bankrupt, because there is no amount of returns that can get you back into the football field. The surest way to go bankrupt is to use

## 2.4. BUFFER STRATEGY

leverage. However, the government is the largest debtor in the world, and, being possessed of the monopoly of violence, does coerce all actors to bolster its position. You can always expect the creditors to be taken advantage of by the debtors in the long run. Whether you want to tempt fate and face the volatility tax to ride the coat tails of the government is a personal decision. I stay away from leverage.

**Drawdowns.** The biggest issue with the asset markets is that they tend to go down suddenly, then gradually creep upward. We eschew risk-adjusted metrics (such as the Sharpe ratio), preferring to separate out the risk as additional information. All models based on the normal distribution have a systematic tendency to underestimate risk – all models that rely on second order moments, for that matter. There is a measure of risk called the Calmar ratio, which was devised for the California pension fund. We use a related measure: the number of years it takes to get back out after experiencing the expected maximum drawdown. Note, again, that both expected maximum drawdown and average return are very, very rough estimates.

**Getting out of the hole.** How long does it take to get back out of a hole? Let's look at the five major down drafts since 1928. We report the drawdown for each year, along with the number of years it took to make ourselves whole, and the number of years it took to get back to the trend of 6% CAGR. All figures are adjusted for dividends and inflation.

|      |                  |          | Years   |          |
| Year | Description      | Drawdown | To even | To trend |
|------|------------------|----------|---------|----------|
| 1929 | Great depression | -8.83%   | 7Y      | 29Y      |
| 1939 | World war II     | -1.10%   | 5Y      | 15Y      |
| 1969 | Stagflation      | -13.60%  | 3Y      | 28Y      |
| 2000 | Dot-com          | -12.01%  | 13Y     | > 21Y    |
| 2008 | Financial Crisis | -36.61%  | 5Y      | 9Y       |

There was no 50 year period that could have avoided those crashes: you will almost certainly see at least one of them in retirement. We can get back to our (inflation-adjusted) capital typically within a decade. Unfortunately, it takes 30 years, or more than half our actuarial life expectancy, to return to the trend line of 6% CAGR. As of 2022, we haven't actually recovered from the dot-com bust in that regard: it's more than a lost decade. In the period from 1966 to 1983, the stock market barely broke even. Time and returns are duals of each other: if you anticipate a 6% annualized return from the stock market, be prepared to wait through three decades of lean years; if you're willing to accept a 3% annualized return, then you may have to wait for about 15 years. Note, finally, that our analysis is based on the realized historical series, without re-sampling, thus underestimating the maximum wait times.

### 2.4.3 Joint stock ownership

So, the past is no guidance for the future. What then? We can forget precise portfolio allocation, because the volatility of assets into the future is unknown. One bad year could wipe out years of above average returns. Let's throw out our spreadsheets for a minute. Can we guesstimate

## 2.4. BUFFER STRATEGY

return rates without using history as a guide?

There is a logical explanation for why we should earn money from capital. We will provide money now to enable productive enterprises to build gizmos and services that will be useful for others, thus returning the capital invested plus extra profit. We do not provide the money directly to those who produce, rather, we mutualize our contribution with other providers of capital in a joint stock ownership scheme. We will share the profits should there be any. The cumulative return is the amalgamation of many factors, including tax rates, failures, and the quality of labor employed.

### Where passive income comes from

Let's look at some asset classes and what returns we could expect from them. Because capital can flow from one place to another more or less freely in most circumstances, each of these asset classes offer a combination of risk and reward that also provides a benchmark to measure the others.

**Gold.** Gold does not produce anything. It has industrial uses, including dental work. Because it is so precious, most gold is said to remain above ground. It is not destroyed. About 2% of the total supply of gold is mined every year. This is balanced by a population growth rate of 1% to 2% per annum. So the amount of gold per capita remains roughly constant. Gold appears to increase in value when we can purchase more goods with the same weight of gold. That happens through productivity improvements. In 1900, 15% of the US population was involved in farming. A century later, we need less than 1% to produce enough food to make 40% of the population overweight. Therefore, a pound of pork should cost less in terms of gold now than it did a century ago. Productivity gains in the US have been estimated to average around 2% in the last decade, implying that gold should gain about 2% in perceived value thanks to process improvements. Note that, in practice, gold can outperform the stock market for decades.

**Corporate bonds.** You can also lend directly to a company. The company will pay you at a pre-arranged fixed rate interest for a period of time, then return your principal. The default rate of high-yield (high risk) corporate bonds varies from 0% to 20% per year. The recovery rate, meaning the amount of recovered after a default was declared, varies between 25% to 70%. Recovery rate tends to be high when default rate is low and vice-versa. So, a break-even rate of 4%-8% excluding inflation is the absolute minimum you should ask for: your money can be tied up in the recovery process for years. I cannot recommend Sydney Homer's *magnum opus*, "A History Of Interest Rates" enough.

| Default rate | Recovery rate | Recovered |
|---|---|---|
| 5% | 25% | $95\% + 5\% \times 25\% = 96\%$ |
| 20% | 60% | $80\% + 20\% \times 60\% = 92\%$ |

**Residential real estate.** Real estate is a special kind of business that is somewhat easier to understand, at a high level. You borrow money at prevailing rates to buy a property. Then, you maintain that property, pay taxes, and find tenants to pay the rent. A vacancy rate, when the property remains unused during maintenance or while you find tenants might look like one month a year. Banks

## 2.4. BUFFER STRATEGY

can choose to lend their money to you, the government, or the average corporate mentioned above. The default rate on mortgages tends to stay below 5%, but shot up to more than 10% during the Global Financial Crisis of 2008. The recovery rate also tends to be fairly high, but is a major headache for banking institutions. Inflation, fueled by reckless governments, will forgive your debt away. If you borrow at 8% with an inflation rate of 3%, you need to make 5% on your property. Assuming a 10% vacancy rate and another 10% of maintenance costs, you need to charge at least 6% of inflation-adjusted rent to have a chance of breaking even.

Now, let's turn to expected returns in shared ownership of a company.

### Equities

Now, let's turn to equity ownership in corporations. You share ownership of an enterprise. The stock market allows people to exchange ownership for money. It is a highly active and closely watched market, and at times absurdly inaccurate. Despite wide fluctuations in stock prices, at heart, there is a real physical process of value creation in which your participate. Let's get a sense of how this works.

**Anatomy of a corporation.** A corporation, broadly speaking, has equity (shareholders), debt, and assets. It uses cash raised from equity and debt to run the business in pursuit of profit. Because of various tax and accounting rules, official statements could be meaningless. Amortization has special tax advantages and tends to undervalue assets. Stock-based liabilities go unreported. Debt maturity and covenants are not disclosed. Analyzing a company's financial position is error-prone.

**The magic of double-entry bookkeeping.** Double-book accounting is like the holy principle of conservation of mass in physics. Money doesn't suddenly appear or disappear from the books. Most popularly known for its adoption by the Medici bank in Florence, the double-book accounting principle records movements of cash on two ledgers: debit (cash in), and credit (cash out). A healthy company will generate profits. They will have to be dispersed to current owners, or stay in the company. Thanks to double-entry bookkeeping, we know that these profits will go to only five categories, namely:

1. Dividends: the extra cash is returned to the owners for them to use as they please. In many cases, there is an implicit promise the dividends will remain at least constant with respect to inflation. This makes the company look like an inflation-protected bond.

2. Buy-backs: shares of the company are retired from circulation, increasing the share of ownership of existing owners. This is similar to dividends, except for tax purposes. Unlike dividends, they tend to be a one-time event with no expectation of recurrence.

3. Investment: the cash is re-invested in the company to develop new products, upgrade plants and equipment, etc. This is a bet on the future of the company.

4. Mergers and acquisitions: the company acquires another related company. A premium is paid above the

## 2.4. BUFFER STRATEGY

current market price. Overwhelmingly, this tends to destroy value.

5. Retained as cash: the cash is used to pay off debts and kept on hand at the company. This is a capital buffer that can be used when credit is tight or cash will be needed at a moment's notice, for instance, for an acquisition. Excessive amounts of cash tend to be destructive of value.

Regulation and the prospects of the corporation dictate how these outlays are allocated. A mature corporation has little prospect for growth, so it will tend to favor dividends over investments.

**Profits stay yours.** So, owners of a company share the profits. They can be distributed immediately, shoved back into accruing the value of a company, which is yours in part. Eventually, you should be able to enjoy the accrual of value, unless bad investment decisions on the part of the management destroy value before you get a chance to realize it.

**Bond with variable coupon.** Ben Graham, the godfather of value investing, was a bond analyst who started studying securities. He contributed the idea that a ownership in a joint stock company could be viewed as buying a perpetual bond with a variable coupon. The variable coupon is the earnings. The coupon tend to increase based on the success of the enterprise. Instead of fixed pay rates, a dividend is distributed.

**Earnings yield.** This is the price you pay. The earnings yield is calculated by dividing the profit stream by the price you pay. It's similar to the price you pay for a bond and can be compared directly to a bond's yield to maturity. As an owner of the business, the earnings can be distributed as dividends or not: the value will still be accrued to your ownership share no matter what. A minimum hurdle rate of 5% should be demanded. Some businesses lose money with no prospects of improvement, yet they still change hands at valuations above their liquidation value. Occasionally, some businesses can trade for less than 30% of their net profits, meaning that in three years you will be made whole.

**Return on capital.** This is the value you get, the quality of the business. For a full analysis, we should be able to project the earnings infinitely into the future. This cannot be done in practice with any accuracy. In the long run, profits will converge to return on capital. The return on capital is the profits divided by the tangible capital employed. This measures the quality of the enterprise. Again, this is comparable to a bond yield. A company should make good use of capital or return the money to its shareholders.

**Returning all profits.** Please note that there is a special kind of company, called Regulated Investment Company (RIC). An RIC must return almost all profits to shareholders every year. They are the closest to mimicking a bond where the coupon matches the earnings. The most well-known are Business Development Corporations and Real Estate Investment Trusts. In exchange for this thinner corporate veil, there are tax advantages.

**Benchmarking against interest rates.** As Warren E. Buffet points out, interest rates are like gravity to equity valuations. We can compare earnings yield and return on capital to bond rates directly. If, discounted for risk,

## 2.4. BUFFER STRATEGY

bonds become more attractive, accomplished capital allocators and lenders will turn to bonds at the expense those equities of lesser prospect.

**Inflation protection.** If inflation were uniform, that is, if prices would be marked up uniformly across the board, then a company's input materials, wages would increase at the same rate as its prices. So, on the whole, profits should be naturally inflation protected. In practice, during periods of high inflation, economic activity is crippled, and society is going back to basics: commodities. Industrial companies that turn commodities into refined products often lack the pricing power to offset increases in cost. As a general rule, stock prices do not perform as well as commodities during periods of high inflation.

### 2.4.4 The delivery problem: maturity mismatch

So, stocks seem to be a superior asset for generating income. Sharing profits rather than lending (bonds) or partaking in general prosperity (gold) has some logic to it. Empirically, there is some indication that equities will outperform other asset classes when the economy is stable.

But it comes with a catch: if you try to take the money out, you may have to wait. Sometimes, it can take a decade for the value of your ownership stake to converge to a fair price. There is no good way to diversify: all stocks tend to suffer from temporarily depressed prices at the same time.

To sustain your lifestyle, you need to take a regular delivery of cash. If your stock portfolio goes up and down, how do you make sure that you will have the money when you need it?

First, you could simply hold cash. Unfortunately, the cash will eventually run out before you die and you will run out of money. Second, you could purchase insurance (a hedge, in financial parlance). Now, the hedge will:

1. Cost some money every year. This is called the "carry", because it's a weight to hold that hedging position. I am aware of only one institution that has a credible negative carry, associated with Nassim Taleb. If we assume stock market average returns to be around 5%, then paying 2% insurance every year, waiting for a 22% payoff every ten years, is psychologically hard to implement.

2. Return some, all, or more than all of the depreciation in stock holdings when a large drawdown is realized.

3. When all is said and done, the carry and insurance payout should balance to a positive return. As it stands, most strategies available to retail investors will have a carry and a negative overall return: in other words, it's not a good deal.

4. Actually pay the insurance money when due. This is called counter-party risk.

Sadly, for the retail investor, hedging risk explicitly is mostly a losing proposition.

### 2.4.5 Strategy

So, here's the buffer strategy. We understand that bad things happen to our portfolio, even diversified. It's not

## 2.4. BUFFER STRATEGY

really the magnitude of a single year that is harmful, it's staying in the doldrums for a long time. Let's imagine that we have a portfolio that will provide, in the long run, an adequate average compounded return. What if we could insulate ourselves from the ups and downs of the market?

We expect a downturn to last, say, for 16 years before the volatile investment portfolio returns to its long-term average. If we can survive that long without touching the investment portfolio, it's as if nothing had happened.

### Dividends and growth

Before we get into the buffer strategy proper, let's take a look at dividends as a source of income. In most studies, we make the assumption that dividends are immediately re-invested in the company without tax. Here, we will instead look at the stock market as a bond whose par value increases over time, and whose coupon varies over time.

Well, it's a bit complex to analyze. First, the returns move the price of the stock up and down. If a recession is about to happen, the face value (price) of cyclical stocks can go down, say by 50%. The dividend yield, that is, the cash layout divided by the price, goes up 100% (doubles). The company, in anticipation of hard times ahead, will reduce its dividend next year somewhat. The Federal Reserve will monetize large fiscal spending to stimulate the economy: that will increase inflation, thus canceling the nominal gains in stock market prices. The dividend is extracted over an inflated stock price, but is itself cheapened by inflation.

Let's take a look at how these for the twenty years after

2000.

| Year | Return | Div Yield | Par gain | Div Yield over par | Cum infl | Yield/par (-infl) |
|---|---|---|---|---|---|---|
| 2000 | -6.84 | 1.22 | -6.84 | 1.14 | -3.28 | 1.10 |
| 2001 | -13.98 | 1.37 | -19.86 | 1.10 | -4.76 | 1.05 |
| 2002 | -21.46 | 1.79 | -37.06 | 1.13 | -6.97 | 1.05 |
| 2003 | 20.18 | 1.61 | -24.36 | 1.22 | -8.69 | 1.11 |
| 2004 | 10.97 | 1.62 | -16.06 | 1.36 | -11.57 | 1.20 |
| 2005 | 5.24 | 1.76 | -11.66 | 1.55 | -14.49 | 1.33 |
| 2006 | 12.23 | 1.76 | -0.86 | 1.74 | -16.61 | 1.46 |
| 2007 | 4.43 | 1.87 | 3.54 | 1.94 | -19.88 | 1.55 |
| 2008 | -40.67 | 3.23 | -38.58 | 1.98 | -19.95 | 1.59 |
| 2009 | 26.53 | 2.02 | -22.28 | 1.57 | -22.07 | 1.22 |
| 2010 | 11.81 | 1.83 | -13.10 | 1.59 | -23.22 | 1.22 |
| 2011 | 0.14 | 2.13 | -12.97 | 1.85 | -25.43 | 1.38 |
| 2012 | 14.39 | 2.20 | -0.45 | 2.19 | -26.71 | 1.61 |
| 2013 | 27.10 | 1.94 | 26.53 | 2.45 | -27.79 | 1.77 |
| 2014 | 13.63 | 1.92 | 43.79 | 2.76 | -28.33 | 1.98 |
| 2015 | -0.01 | 2.11 | 43.77 | 3.03 | -28.85 | 2.16 |
| 2016 | 9.37 | 2.03 | 57.25 | 3.19 | -30.30 | 2.23 |
| 2017 | 18.59 | 1.84 | 86.49 | 3.43 | -31.74 | 2.34 |
| 2018 | -3.64 | 2.09 | 79.70 | 3.76 | -33.02 | 2.52 |
| 2019 | 25.84 | 1.83 | 126.12 | 4.14 | -34.52 | 2.71 |
| 2020 | 16.27 | 1.58 | 162.90 | 4.15 | -35.39 | 2.68 |

The table has the following columns:

1. Year: the year in question.

2. Return: the year-on-year stock market return.

3. Div Yield: the dividend yield.

## 2.4. BUFFER STRATEGY

4. Par gain: the cumulative gain in stock price since Jan 1, 2000.

5. Div Yield over par: the dividend yield, but measured over the initial investment in 2000.

6. Cum infl: cumulative inflation up to that year. So, in 2020, it was 35%. That means that if you kept $100 under the mattress since 2000, at the end of 2020, that $100 would afford you $65 worth of goods.

7. Yield/par (-infl): the dividend yield over par, corrected for inflation (so-called "real").

All values are in percentage except the year. The dividend is not corrected for stock buybacks, which is a tax-efficient way (mostly) to distribute dividends that has gained wide spread practice in the last decade.

Let's assume you invested $100 in 2000. You consume the dividend as it comes out every year. It's been steadily increasing to more than double over time. The stock market value has stayed roughly flat: $162 \times (100 - 35) = 105$. The face value of the dividend yield has increased slowly but stayed roughly between 1.6% and 2.1%.

Let's repeat the same exercise in a different macro environment:

| Year | Return | Div Yield | Par gain | Div Yield over par | Cum infl | Yield/par (-infl) |
|---|---|---|---|---|---|---|
| 1965 | 9.25 | 2.97 | 9.25 | 3.24 | -1.88 | 3.18 |
| 1966 | -11.34 | 3.53 | -3.13 | 3.42 | -5.17 | 3.24 |
| 1967 | 17.18 | 3.06 | 13.51 | 3.47 | -7.96 | 3.20 |
| 1968 | 11.75 | 2.88 | 26.85 | 3.65 | -12.11 | 3.21 |
| 1969 | -14.45 | 3.47 | 8.52 | 3.77 | -17.24 | 3.12 |
| 1970 | -1.16 | 3.49 | 7.25 | 3.74 | -21.61 | 2.93 |
| 1971 | 10.13 | 3.10 | 18.12 | 3.66 | -24.09 | 2.78 |
| 1972 | 18.48 | 2.68 | 39.95 | 3.75 | -26.59 | 2.75 |
| 1973 | -19.34 | 3.57 | 12.89 | 4.03 | -32.48 | 2.72 |
| 1974 | -29.24 | 5.37 | -20.12 | 4.29 | -39.89 | 2.58 |
| 1975 | 32.25 | 4.15 | 5.65 | 4.38 | -43.79 | 2.46 |
| 1976 | 18.04 | 3.87 | 24.70 | 4.83 | -46.40 | 2.59 |
| 1977 | -10.39 | 4.98 | 11.74 | 5.56 | -49.76 | 2.80 |
| 1978 | 2.44 | 5.28 | 14.47 | 6.04 | -53.92 | 2.79 |
| 1979 | 12.16 | 5.24 | 28.39 | 6.73 | -59.33 | 2.74 |
| 1980 | 23.84 | 4.61 | 59.00 | 7.33 | -63.85 | 2.65 |

We experienced high inflation during Arthur Burns at the Federal Reserve, and President Nixon severed the last remains of gold convertibility in 1971. The face value of Treasury yields went into double digits. Over that period, the stock market (without dividend re-investment but inflation-adjusted) went, at best nowhere. In 1975 your ten-year run would have lost you 38% in real terms, while the face value increased by 5%. The dividend yield, back then, was fairly decent.

From these experiences, you can think about how policy response and the economy affects income extracted from dividends. Broadly speaking, an increase in stock market value reflects a business that is growing. A relatively high

## 2.4. BUFFER STRATEGY

dividend yield reflects a preference for short term cash: businesses find it harder to find good profitable investment opportunities and return capital to shareholders. On the whole, you could see that the dividend tends to be less volatile than stock market prices. Stock market prices reflect compounding expectations for decades into the future. Since they are very uncertain, they move around a lot. Dividends, on the other hand, represent a share of cash extracted from real businesses minus investments. On aggregate, even during wars and lockdowns, the real economy continues as people go to work to transport food and build things for each other. There are secular changes due to government policy (tax, fiscal stimulus), demographics, geopolitics, energy cycles, and other factors that tend to have an effect slowly over time.

### Surviving the lean years

How do we, then, provide for our living expenses during the 16 lean years?

Let's say we estimated a withdrawal rate of 3.33% to pay for living expenses. So the portfolio should be 30 years worth of living expenses. Now, let's for a moment imagine we keep 16 years worth of a cookie jar for the lean years. We'd have 14 years left to put in investment securities. Assuming a rate of 3.33% of real returns on that portfolio, we're just breaking even: after the first 14 years, we'd have run out of investment, so overall, we would only survive 30 years with that money. We need 10 to 20 more years to survive in retirement.

Let us say that $P$ is the size of the portfolio, in living

expense years, including the cash buffer. Let's call $r$ the investment average compounded returns adjusted for inflation. $D(r)$ is the number of years in the downturn to get back to the $r$ trend line, which we match to the inflation-protected cash buffer. Call $Y$ the total number years in retirement. If we die exactly destitute, and assuming that there is one downturn, it's as if the investment portfolio had a constant CAGR of $r$, and we can add to that the cash buffer:

$$Y = [P - D(r)](1+r)^{(P-D(r))} + D(r).$$

Instead of solely relying on cash as a buffer, we'll tap into the dividend stream. During lean years, we assume the dividends of surviving companies to adjust for inflation. Companies which provide staples and health, constants come rain or shine, are assumed to have stable profits in the absence of government intervention. We expect dividends to shrink by, say, 25% during a crisis, then we have to provision an additional 33%. You will lose the returns from re-investing the dividend.

So, let's say we want to survive the lean years using 50% from dividends and 50% from cash reserves. Further, let's assume the lean years to last for approximately 16 years. Next, let's consider the case where our living expenses are 3% of the original portfolio, so that, in hard times, dividends will provide for 1.5%. Assume, further, that we have a $3m portfolio with $90k yearly spend. All percentages in the following table are in relation to the total portfolio, including the buffer, except the "dividend yield".

|  | % of total | Value |
|---|---|---|
| Total portfolio | 100% | $3m |
| Yearly spend | 3% | $90k |
| 8 years of cash reserves | 8 × 3% = 24% | $720k |
| Investable portfolio | 76% | $2.28m |
|  | Yield | Value |
| Dividend required | 1.5% × 33% = 2% | $60k |
| Dividend during lean years | 2% × 75% = 1.5% | $45k |
| Dividend yield | 2% / 76% = 2.6% | $60k |
|  | % of total | Return |
| Yield on cash | 24% | 0% |
| Total return on non-cash | 76% | 4% |

The cash reserves could be invested in a 16-year ladder inflation-protected bond. During lean years, instead of rolling expiring rungs of the ladder as they expire, we spend the principal, shortening the average duration until funds are depleted. It is not advisable to extend the maximum maturity to the full 16 years because we are taking inflation risk: instead, stay around 5 years.

So, we need to keep approximately 25% of the portfolio in cash, then keep the remaining assets in a high dividend portfolio, or, when a crisis hit, reshuffle into a 3%-yield portfolio, taking the tax hit. As the portfolio grows, the cash proportion gradually diminishes as the spending remains constant.

## 2.5 Summary

It's been a long chapter. Thank you for sticking until the end! Let's see what topics we broached.

Firstly, we looked at once-in-a-lifetime **existential threats**.

We introduced a framework to **categorize** them, and various methodologies for identifying a chronology or a sequence to **anticipate** what is approaching. We showed some **examples** drawn from history. We identified **consequences** to your day-to-day life. We showed some potential **reactions** to avoid the *tabula rasa*. History is fascinating, but don't expect historical moments to happen every year of your life. Something big will almost certainly happen once, the kind that requires unconventional asset protection measures, but it won't happen every day. No need to live in the bunker, but memorize the escape route to the bunker for that time when seconds can save your life.

Secondly, we looked at financial planning through the **classical** lens. We saw how to approach forecasting of your **spending rate** throughout your life. We analyzed the rules that dictate **how much** you can spend given the size of your portfolio. We described **portfolio allocation** as a means to resolve asset maturity mismatch and the volatility tax. In classical financial planning, **failure**, meaning, running out of money prior to death, is presented as a probability, with no further analysis. The attitude is essentially: tough luck. You can be more resilient by managing inter-generational relationships and cultivating the ability to retract into basic level subsistence.

Finally, we reviewed the **Buffer Strategy**. We start by observing that **fat tail** distributed variables, such as stock market prices, cannot be analyzed with regular mathematical tools on which classical financial planning are based. We measure **risk as time to recover** after the largest loss. We forgo most statistical analysis and rely on reasoning to justify investment in different **asset classes** such as stocks, bonds, gold, and real estate. The buffer strategy aims to resolve the **maturity mismatch** of when we need the money and fluctuations in the stock market. We survive during **16 lean years** with a combination of cash and dividends. With this strategy, fluctuation in the stock market can be ignored.

## 2.6 Reading further

### 2.6.1 Resilience

 **The House of Rothschild by Niall Ferguson.** If you have time, this multi-volume goes into depth into the Rothschild's fortunes over the centuries. The family dealt with government bonds. While they did certainly lose their place in the top concentrators of wealth, they demonstrated that you could survive a world war, being persecuted in the country of your first branch and occupied in all branches but one. As a bond dealer, surviving occupation of all major powers, expropriation, hyperinflation, is no small feat. Niall Ferguson never fails to deliver his legendary erudition.

 **You can farm: the entrepreneur's guide to start and succeed in a farming enterprise by Joel Salatin.** If you want to own and cultivate land, this book is a primer for farm management. You could hire help to till the land. It is describes soil and crop selection and other practical matters you need to understand before buying the land.

 **In the Wake of the Plague: The Black Death and the World It Made by Norman F. Cantor.** The pre-eminent historian on the Middle Ages takes a closer look at the century of the Black Death and famines, and its social implications. Highly recommended.

## 2.6. READING FURTHER

**So You've Been Publicly Shamed by Jon Ronson.** In this era of wokism, you could be outed by the mob within seconds. It doesn't matter if the accusations were anywhere close to correct. There is no due process, and no notion of proportionality. It will take years to repair your reputation. This book shows what to do. Highly recommended if you have an online presence.

### 2.6.2 Sea change

**The Civil War by Julius Caesar.** Only tangentially relevant today, the Civil War is a first-hand account of the civil war that ultimately engulfed the Roman Republic. Caesar also wrote The Conquest of Gaul, which details the military subjugation and ethnic cleansing of what is France today. It is well-written.

 **The grand strategy of the Byzantine Empire by Edward Luttwak.** Contrary to all expectations, the Eastern Roman empire managed to survive for a thousand years longer than Rome. Composite reflex bows and horses gave marauding tribes military superiority which limited its power. It was the asymmetric warfare of the day. Like with the Chinese empires, some amount negotiation and divide-and-conquer with neighboring tribes helped the empire survive.

 **A history of interest rates by Sydney Homer (maintained by Richard Scylla).** Sydney Homer used to work for Solomon Brothers, the premier bond trading outfit in the 80s, until it blew up under the tutelage of John Meriwether (who went on to create Long Term Capital Management, and JWM Partners, which also blew up). This is a **must-read**. It chronicles interest rates starting before money was created until the

## 2.6. READING FURTHER

present day.

 **Diplomacy by Henry Kissinger.** Say what you will about the results of his policies, this book is the most lucid account of foreign policy from the 16th century onward. This is a **must-read**.

 **7 deadly scenarios by Andrew Krepinevich.** Andrew Krepinevich reviews how the Pentagon thinks in scenarios that could go wrong. This book was written in 2010. The world functions with an incredible amount of trust. If nothing else, you will come away feeling grateful to be alive. This is a **must-read**.

**On war by Carl von Clausewitz.** It was said that it is a book well-known, but little read. This book informs military strategy in the United States. At the time, von Clausewitz, on the Prussian side, was overshadowed by Baron de Jomini, on the Napoleonic side. Von Clausewitz views war as the furtherance of political objectives by other means.

**Century: One Hundred Years of Human Progress, Regression, Suffering and Hope published by Bruce Bernard and Terence McNamee** This is a **must-read**. It has 100 pages, one for each year from 1900 to 2000. It's an efficient way to give you a visual perspective of what can happen in a century. Small events that were large at the time, and small progress compounded over a century. You will live to see the next half of this book! This is a **must-read**.

## 2.6. READING FURTHER

 **Civilization: The West and the Rest by Niall Ferguson.** While unnecessarily seeking to be more abrasive and condescending to pique interest, this book nevertheless raises the point that the unprecedented success that we had in the last two centuries was not entirely an accident. It relied on sound institutions and cultural elements. If you believe that the West is all but done, think again.

 **Guns, Germs, and Steel: The Fates of Human Societies by Jared Diamond.** In his seminal book, Jared Diamond attempts to elucidate the reasons of the supremacy of the West. It is perhaps the first book of its kind and still worth a read.

 **Collapse: How Societies Choose to Fail or Succeed by Jared Diamond.** This book aims to find clues on how leadership brings societies to ruin. Perhaps unsurprisingly, exploitative practices ultimately result in poor results in the long run. The study does not provide a comprehensive and systematic approach, and does have a political agenda.

 **Upheaval: Turning Points for Nations in Crisis by Jared Diamond.** Another book by Jared Diamond, this attempts to find the pivotal triggers that cause sudden downfalls.

## 2.6. READING FURTHER

 **Destined for War: Can America and China Escape Thucydides's Trap? by Graham Allison.** This book draws a parallel between Pericles and today. It argues that most transitions out of leadership are violent, in short because the hegemony does not want to yield. It's not clear to me that the transition is imminent, thought it seems quite likely that some new world order will emerge within my lifetime.

 **Mao's Great Famine by Frank Dikötter.** This book studies the impact of Mao's reforms on China. Bar pandemics, man-made disasters claim the most lives.

 **Nothing to Envy: Ordinary Lives in North Korea by Barbara Demick.** The heart-wrenching story of Korean families that were boiled like the proverbial frog in North Korea, and the unimaginable cost of defection. Now, owing to surveillance in China, defection is no longer a viable option. This book is a **must-read.**

 **Krakatoa: The Day the World Exploded, August 27, 1883 by Simon Winchester.** A well-researched account of the Krakatoa eruption that led to the year without summer. The economic implications are probably not as important as the book suggests. Still, this was an extraordinary event.

## 2.6. READING FURTHER

**False Alarm: How Climate Change Panic Costs Us Trillions, Hurts the Poor, and Fails to Fix the Planet by Bjorn Lomborg.** There is no doubt that we could have managed a better energy transition. We have wasted trillions and will probably waste a few trillions more. But in the end, we will have to adopt what works.

**For Good and Evil: The Impact of Taxes on the Course of Civilization by Charles Adams.** A masterful review of tax regimes internationally and throughout history. Charles Adams was a libertarian tax lawyer. You can find the audio of his engaging presentations on the von Mises institute. If you have an interest in taxes, this is a **must-read**.

**The End Is Always Near: Apocalyptic Moments, from the Bronze Age Collapse to Nuclear Near Misses by Dan Carlin.** This book resets your expectation of how close we live to a major disaster.

**The Storm Before the Storm: The Beginning of the End of the Roman Republic by Mike Duncan.** For those history buffs out there, this is a blow-by-blow account of the drama that led to the civil war. It was a long time coming.

**End Times: A Brief Guide**

## 2.6. READING FURTHER

**to the End of the World by Bryan Walsh.** My section on taxonomy of disaster was largely inspired by this book. This is a **must-read**.

 **Risk: A User's Guide by General Stanley McChrystal and Anna Butrico.** The military, in most countries, spends 95% of their time reflecting on what could go, and did go wrong; they prepare for the unexpected. The US military has a lot of first rate thinkers. Resilience when predictions are inane is a good posture to have. Preparing without a plan will work in all situations.

 **The Little Ice Age: How Climate Made History 1300-1850 by Brian Fagan.** We think about global warming with apprehension. Currently, however, deaths from cold exceed those from warmth by a factor of 7. We may learn from a period of cold weather that lasted for half a millennium.

 **The Unthinkable: Who Survives When Disaster Strikes - and Why by Amanda Ripley.** A thorough study of how people deal with disaster. People act in strange ways under stress. This a **must-read**.

 **Until Proven Safe: The History and Future of Quarantine by Nicola Twilley, Geoff Manaugh.** The studies that are slowly trickling in show that lockdowns were ineffective. It doesn't mean that it was a poor decision (initially), and it certainly doesn't mean that the government will do it again, amped up, if presented with the opportunity of using the god-like powers of a national emergency.

## 2.6. READING FURTHER

 **The Rational Optimist: How Prosperity Evolves by Matt Ridley.** It's easy to focus on what goes wrong. In doing so, you might miss on the upside. This is to remind us that things go right all the time.

 **The Precipice: Existential Risk and the Future of Humanity by Toby Ord.** A philosopher examines extinction-level possibilities. There's a class of events that cannot be prevented, and whose outcomes cannot be mitigated. When making plans, this realization should instill a sense of urgency and place a limit on the delay of gratification.

### 2.6.3 Mechanics

**Capitalism, Socialism and Democracy by Joseph Schumpeter.** Schumpeter is well-known for his business cycle theory. There was a time when economists, particularly Austrian economists, would discuss macro-economic issues at the boundary of freedom and prosperity. He coined the term "creative destruction".

**The Great Reflation by J. Anthony Boeckh.** Written in 2010 as a retrospective of the response to the Global Financial Crisis, this books gives some insight into the mechanics of the money printing that "saved" the system. Tony Boeckh works at Alpine Macro.

## 2.6. READING FURTHER

 **This Time Is Different by Carmen Reinhart and Kenneth Rogoff.** The book was published based on faulty calculations, which weaken but do not fundamentally change the conclusions. I recommend you go directly to Prof. Rogoff's Harvard page for the data. The book holds that a debt-to-GDP above 100% will lead to a major crisis for the countries which flirt with it.

 **Oil 101 by Morgan Downey.** If you want to understand the mechanics of the oil market, netback pricing, what light sweet crude means and why a barrel of oil is larger than a regular barrel, look no further. Highly recommended.

 **Money, bank credit and economic cycles by Jesus Huerta de Soto.** If you need a primer on Austrian economics, this is it. Highly recommended.

 **Dying of Money by Jens O. Parssons (Ronald Marcks).** Written in the 1970s, this book revisits the German and American inflations. This is a **must-read**.

 **When Money Dies by Adam Ferguson.** Adam Ferguson effectively describes the German inflation with boots on the ground, as it were. It's

## 2.6. READING FURTHER

relatable and reifies the statistics to day-to-day life. This is a **must-read**.

 **Economics of Inflation: A Study of Currency Depreciation in Post-War Germany by Costantino Bresciani-Turroni.** A comprehensive analysis of inflation in Germany from the perspective of an economic statistician. Highly recommended.

 **CPM precious metal yearbooks.** If you want to learn about the gold or silver markets, look no further. It details production, industrial uses, and deep analysis of the gold and silver markets. The book is published for gold and silver and updated every year. The book price appears to be pegged to the money supply. This is a **must-read**.

 **Moneyland: The Inside Story of the Crooks and Kleptocrats Who Rule the World by Oliver Bullough.** There seems to be a special zone for those who have resources, not only thieves but also people with legitimate reasons to seek shelter for their wealth. Highly recommended.

 **The Civilization of the Middle Ages by Norman F. Cantor.** In his magnum opus, Norman Cantor revisits the Middle Ages through the lens of the investiture conflict (the attempt of the Archbishop of Rome to seize temporal power from the Emperor), and Veblen's theory of conspicuous consumption. If you're dying to understand how the Church got involved in weddings, this is your long-winded answer. Highly recommended.

## 2.6. READING FURTHER

 **Spain: The Centre of the World 1519-1682 by Robert Goodwin.** This books is about Spain, the first global power. It's a familiar story of rise and fall.

 **The Rise and Fall of the Great Powers: Economic Change and Military Conflict from 1500 to 2000 by Paul Kennedy.** The fall from grace of the hegemon always comes from attempting to preserve an untenable position. Usually, military might is supported beyond what the economy can support.

 **When China Rules the World:**

**The End of the Western World and the Birth of a New Global Order by Martin Jacques.** One of the most influential political analysts of his day, Martin Jacques walks us through the process of Chinese ascendancy that is unfolding before our eyes.

**Principles for Dealing with the Changing World Order: Why Nations Succeed or Fail by Ray Dalio.** Best known for running the world's biggest macro hedge fund, Ray Dalio tracks various proprietary metrics to show that China is going to displace the US for first place. The transition could be painful, as we know from Thucydides' trap. The book is full of interesting and relevant statistics. Take the conclusions with a pinch of salt, particularly on the timing of events. Highly recommended.

### 2.6.4 Economics and finance

 **Retirement Planning Guidebook: Navigating the Important Decisions for Retirement Success by Wade Pfau.** The most comprehensive and easily digestible compendium of classical retirement planning. This is a great way to read all his blog posts as one coherent whole. This is a **must-read**.

 **Time and money by Roger Garrison.** Roger Garrison was a trained electrical engineer. He describes Austrian economics with figures and graphs for the visually minded. He compares Keynes and Hayek theories on capital structures.

**Security analysis - 6th edition by Benjamin Graham, and David Dodd.** Warren Buffett recommends reading the sixth edition. The critical insight is that an equity can be viewed as a perpetual bond with variable coupon. That provides a bridge between the bond and equities market. It predates Michael Milken's bond revolution by half a century.

**Tomorrow's Gold by Marc Faber.** A Swiss economist who worked for Drexel Asia during their heyday, Dr. Marc Faber gives us an entertaining, masterful view of international economic history until the present, where he predicts the rise of Asia. This is a **must-read**.

## 2.6. READING FURTHER

**The War Ledger by Kigler Organski and Jacek Kugler.** From the reparations burden that saddled Germany and led to hyperinflation and the World War II, we know that wars cost a lot. Ultimately, this wanton destruction of lives and wealth will be a burden borne by victors and vanquished alike. People talk about stimulative effects of the war machine, but in fact it is just the government appropriating resources for itself to destroy the product outright.

**America's Bank: The Epic Struggle to Create the Federal Reserve by Roger Lowenstein.** The feud between Alexander Hamilton and Thomas Jefferson ended in the establishment of the first central bank. This conflict also set the stage for the peculiar legal status where corporations are almost as people (see "We, the corporations"). It was a monster then, and it is a monster now.

 **Common Sense on Mutual Funds: New Imperatives for the Intelligent Investor by John C. Bogle.** You probably don't need a reason to invest in index funds. If you do, this is from the man who created them.

 **Enough: True Measures of Money, Business, and Life by John C. Bogle.** Jack Bogle lived frugally. This is a retrospective on his life and how to prioritize money and ethical conduct. Enough said.

 **Quit Like a Millionaire: No Gimmicks, Luck, or Trust Fund Required by Kristy**

## 2.6. READING FURTHER

**Shen, Bryce Leung, JL Collins.** A practical guide similar to this book, in approachable, plain English. Don't follow blindly. Highly recommended.

**A Thousand Barrels a Second: The Coming Oil Break Point and the Challenges Facing an Energy Dependent World by Peter Tertzkian.** Written before the shale boom, this book predicted a peak oil uh-oh moment which didn't happen. It shows the correlation between economic activity (GDP - gross domestic product) and oil consumption. It's an almost exact linear relationship prior to the 1970s. After that, Switzerland and Japan were able to break free from this relationship. This is a **must-read**.

**The Little Book of Sideways Markets: How to Make Money in Markets that Go Nowhere by Vitaliy N. Katsenelson.** This book introduced me to the observation that it takes a decade to repair

a typical drawdown, much longer than I had thought. The book argues that sideways markets are the norm. Highly recommended.

**How Asia Works: Success and Failure in the World's Most Dynamic Region by Joe Studwell.** This is a great primer on the Asian models if you aren't familiar with how the region works, and the difference between the Northern economies (think Japan and South Korea) that boomed and the Southern (think Laos) that were left behind. If you don't know what a Zaibatsu or a Chaebol is, this is a **must-read**.

**Safe Haven: Investing for Financial Storms by Mark Spitznagel.** Probably the only sound hedging strategy available today. While somewhat long-winded, he gives a good intuitive explanation of the volatility tax. Spitznagel was the head trader for Nassim Taleb. Unfortunately, I am at pains to find a zero

## 2.6. READING FURTHER

carry options strategy. It appears to require some skill of which I am not possessed. Highly recommended.

 **Statistical Consequences of Fat Tails: Real World Preasymptotics, Epistemology, and Applications by Nassim Taleb.** If you are technically minded, this book will speak more to you than his other books. A little less polished, this is a basic review of Lévy stable distributions. Most importantly, it shows that which tools used in conventional statistical processing are inadequate, whatever the fudging factor. If you are technical, this is a **must-read**.

 **The Frackers: The Outrageous Inside Story of the New Billionaire Wildcatters by Gregory Zuckerman.** When everyone took Hubbert's peak to be all be inevitable, a handful of adventurers transformed the United States from the largest importer of oil to the large exporter. They made the impos-

sible happen. The American entrepreneurial spirit never ceases to amaze. A very engaging story as always by Zuckerman.

 **Why Nations Fail: The Origins of Power, Prosperity, and Poverty by Daron Acemoglu, James A. Robinson.** While definitely a partial view of the world, this book does point out benefits of well-functioning institution in a well-function society.

 **A Random Walk Down Wall Street: A Time-Tested Strategy for Successful Investing by Burton G. Malkiel.** A classic that doesn't seem to age.

# Chapter 3

# Health

This chapter is about health. In **finance**, we've covered how to provide material resources to survive. In the next chapter, **purpose**, we'll see how to live with purpose. In this chapter, we're looking at keeping the body and mind working well.

## 3.1 In this chapter

Firstly, we need to define our goal. Should we prioritize health or longevity? That is, which is more important, how long we live or how well we live? We'll cover what living healthy means and how much life extension we can reasonably expect, so that we can choose which aspect is more significant to us.

Secondly, we'll have to understand what will happen to us. We review what can fail. We take a short look at the history medical progress, such as it is. We have some expectations for the future of medical progress which could make our task easier. Do we believe futurologists who predict the end of mortality?

Thirdly, we can see what actions we can take. We need a way to evaluate progress. We can then see what behavior can reach the desired outcome.

Fourthly, we briefly review the basic of mental health. Mental hygiene today is still in its infancy. It is not a discipline per se, but rather comes as a byproduct of other healthy routines.

## 3.2 Goal: actuarial or actual years

We explored finance as a means to provide material means to support our life throughout retirement. Likewise, health will help us preserve our body and mind. The body is a support system for the brain, which houses the senses, including the mind. Maintenance and care of the body is not an end in and of itself. The senses are the interface to the external world. A degraded experience spoils our experience.

We derive pleasure and pain through the body. Over time, the senses dull and decay, while pain tends to increase. The sudden removal of a sense or a simple function can be debilitating.

So, our goal is to preserve the functions of the body in good order for the longest time possible. By functioning well, we mean, ordered roughly by priority:

1. **Mental clarity**: to enjoy a happy life, I believe it's best to keep your wits about. Happiness is a trained ability, and without some basic level of control, you

## 3.2. GOAL: ACTUARIAL OR ACTUAL YEARS

are unable to develop it. Intoxicants, particularly sedatives, detract you from the enjoyment.

2. **Pain-free existence**: bad backs, knee injuries, gout will plague you in your old years. Best avoid activities that may result in a permanent loss of function.

3. **Freedom** (lack of dependence): if you can't feed yourself, or need assistance to go to the toilet, then you will be at the mercy of caregivers. Everyone has their pride.

4. **Dignity**: there is great joy associated with controlling your movements with grace and dignity. If you keep that up in your sunset years, it will be enough.

5. **Survival functions**: in certain situations, the ability to run away, swim to a safer shore, will literally save your life. It's good to maintain a basic level of mobility and strength for potentially unusual situations.

6. **Experience pleasure**: let's be honest: it's the focus for most of us, most of the time. The good food, good music, and all else occupy our thoughts from birth to death.

You may have different priorities, but once your priorities are established, you must act accordingly. It is all too common to see the pursuit of a momentary pleasure jeopardize survival and risk a life-long painful injury.

A well-functioning body will tend to last long, but not always. We would like to preserve the body for as long as we can live a happy life. Suppose we did everything right: what is the upside for life extension, realistically? 5 to 10 years? If we are able to extend our life by 10 years, in good condition, then we're talking about a 20% extension in retirement. It also takes time to achieve this goal, say 5%-10% of our usable hours in the day. In my view, pursuing longevity in and of itself, rather than a byproduct of a well-function body, is simply not worth it. There are activities that have a better return of happiness on time invested.

Upkeep has cost in time and resources, and therefore, the goal should be adding life to our years, not years to our life. Our goal should be the **health span**, the amount of time we are healthy and able to enjoy life.

## 3.3 In the long run

We all know how the story ends: your demise. In the meanwhile, it's a long downward sloping curve. Will medicine cure aging, sickness and death in the interim? Let's find out.

### 3.3.1 Suffer then die

People in the modern world no longer believe in rebirth or the after-life. It's not really death they're afraid about, it's the transition. Pleasure and pain are experienced through the six senses. The senses decay as we age. They are as follows:

- **Mind**: everything you can experience goes through

## 3.3. IN THE LONG RUN

the mind. It is the most essential. However, it is the most robust. Until we find what causes mental degenerative diseases, just monitoring your mental faculties is all the upkeep you need.

- **Sight**: your eyes are precious, and follow a predictable pattern of decay. They are quite delicate, and sudden loss of sight can be damning. Many people who live very old go through their later years almost blind.

- **Touch**: herein we include the ability to ambulate through the world. As lepers can attest, the sense of touch and pain is required. It is quite robust.

- **Hearing**: like sight, hearing tends to decay slowly over time, with individual differences but in a somewhat predictable fashion. There is nothing much you can do to extend your good years of hearing.

- **Taste**: the intensity of the experience decays over time. In the normal course of a lifetime, we are able to experience almost exclusively pleasurable experience through taste. It is not essential for survival in this day and age.

- **Smell**: likewise, the ability to experience smell tends to decay over time, but it is not essential. Like hearing, it cannot be turned off.

As mentioned before, make sure you maintain your body to retain autonomy in your later years. This is probably the most important.

Manage your life well, avoid car accidents, ward off meeting your end at the hands of an unscrupulous robber, manicure your every body muscle at the yoga studio daily, and congratulations! You will die of cancer.

### 3.3.2 From Galen to Pasteur

When you get your next haircut at the barber, look at the barber sign. If you're lucky to live in a place where there is no prohibition against animated signs, you can see the real thing: it's a spinning roll of three colors – red, white, and blue. The colors were introduced in Amsterdam in 1540. They were an indication of what services you could expect at the establishment. Red meant blood letting. White meant setting bones (chiropractors) or pulling teeth, and blue stood for cutting hair. And for a millennium, between the end of the Roman Principate and the Industrial Age, that was basically the state-of-the-art in medical practice. Draw blood, crack bones.

I recommend picking up a copy of "The Emperor of All Maladies" by Siddharta Mukherjee and and "A History of Medicine" by Douglas Guthrie. We've made great progress in sanitation and child mortality. Vaccines eradicated many of the diseases we brought on ourselves with our urban lifestyle. But, by and large, progress in interventions, to the notable exception of CPR, has been almost nil. In fact, if you read "Overdiagnosed" by H. Gilbert Welsh, Lisa Schwartz, and Steven Woloshin, you will understand that medical intervention today, on the whole, is a net negative for most people. Sure, we understand more as we go, but what kind of pace of progress do we expect medicine

## 3.3. IN THE LONG RUN 129

to do in our lifetime? Crack the problem of aging and mortality? Cure blindness?

**Pater, peccavi.** When you go to a Catholic confession, you start the conversation with "Father, forgive me for I have sinned. It's been too long since my last confession." In 2019, prior to my retirement, I went for a check-up and blood test. It was only the second time in the last twenty years that I saw a doctor. It had been both a matter of a deep mistrust in the medical establishment and a result of simply not having the time. Waiting for the doctor, thoughts of atonement were running through my mind: eating with abandon, never exercising. She kept her calm and simply asked whether I was eating a diversified diet. Oftentimes, simple common sense behavior is the best medicine you can get.

### 3.3.3 Outlook

The advancements in medical science today are simply astounding. We can make blind people see. Surgical operations can be performed remotely, or by a robot. We developed the covid-19 vaccine within months. We can edit DNA. Palliative care, commonly understood to have started in 1948 by Cicely Saunders, has effectively eradicated pain.

While there are reasons to be optimistic, it must be acknowledged that transitioning from lab to practice can take decades. There are regulatory issues. Then, we must overcome cost, reliability, and ethical considerations. I have been puzzled by the lack of advances from the quantified self movement (rebranded as biohacking to denote active experimentation). Given these reasons, I anticipate that there will be virtually no meaningful progress that will be available cheaply enough when I need them. Consequently, the best strategy is to assume that you have to care for your mind and body today the same way you did since time immemorial. As mentioned before, the requirement for a human caretaker in most cases poses a huge problem: if solved, it would be a substantial breakthrough. Take hearing aids, which are basically sound amplifiers in your ear: at some point, hearing will deteriorate to the point where a direct nerve connection, and possibly restorative surgery for the nerves themselves. That's much more difficult than what we have today. Here is my evaluation of potential advancements over the next 50 years. As a technologist, I tend to be optimistic.

## 3.3. IN THE LONG RUN

|  | Probability |
|---|---|
| Perfect teeth | 90% |
| Perfect heart | 80% |
| Perfect hearing | 30% |
| Exoskeletons for elderly | 30% |
| Artificial arms and legs | 10% |
| Eliminate human caretaker | 10% |
| Perfect sight | 5% |
| Artificial smell and taste | 5% |
| Artificial hands | 5% |
| Live in the matrix | 5% |
| Perfect sleep | 3% |
| Cure aging | 0% |
| Increase lifespan by 20+ years | 0% |
| Cure all major cancers | 0% |

Advances depend on their difficulty and usefulness. For instance, artificial smell is both difficult and ranked as less useful than, say, vision, so I don't expect there to be much work devoted unless a massive entertainment value can be unlocked. Sight, for instance, probably needs more than 10 years since first commercial application to be reliable. Then, it's likely that it would be prioritized for the fewer otherwise healthy young adults until it comes to the massive population of the elderly. So, take a decade for each of lab development, permitting, commercial application, commoditization, you're talking 40 years until it can be useful for you. Think about how long it took for laser eye surgery to become somewhat reliable. I wouldn't count on fully artificial senses anytime soon.

To counterbalance this, there is a significant possibility that we may discover substantial toxicity, enough to create abnormally elevated levels of cancer, say, in water, foods or cookware that we consider safe today. Sugar ought to be acknowledged as the harmful drug that it is.

## 3.4 Grooming physical health

Now that we know what can go wrong, and what help we can expect from advances in science, is there a change in behavior that can help us live better and longer?

> **You won't live longer if you quit smoking, it only seems longer.** I have a way to delay your death almost indefinitely, and cheaply: cryogenics. If you are spending too much time or developing mental stress in your quest for better health, you're doing it wrong.

Happy people are healthier. They don't need alcohol or drugs, don't saturate their body with cortisol, etc. Mental health has benefits and will be covered in the next section.

To care for your body, you should: sleep well, eat well, exercise, and be prepared for extreme situations. As with finance, you should be aware that there is a tail risk for debilitating events.

Unfortunately, science is not helpful here. Of necessity, experimentation has a lot of regulatory hurdles and is expensive. That makes large studies impractical. Therefore, commercial interest is needed to back studies. In smaller sample sizes, we have to restrict ourselves to single-factor effects (a curse for all) because the curse of dimensionality increases sample size exponentially. In most cases, effects

## 3.4. GROOMING PHYSICAL HEALTH

are relatively small, so we require even large sample sizes. I believe that there are large individual differences, which require slicing and dicing of the samples, that is, inherently, there are no single factor effects. The quantified self movement was meant to lower regulatory and ethical constraints by encouraging self-experimentation, but it never achieved the rigor of lab science, neither were results shared widely, nor had made reliable technology available for the mass market. To some extent, it is a chicken and egg problem. The EEG sleep monitors failed because they lacked actionable insights, which hindered their success.

Therefore, I will report my own experience here. In the absence of strict experimentation, it is anecdotal and poorly measured. Frankly, only yoga, meditation and low-carb dieting seem to help. This is a current snapshot of my protocols and subject to change frequently.

### 3.4.1 Evaluation metrics

**If you can't measure it, you can't improve it.** Attributed to Lord Kelvin, the idea is that we need metrics to track progress. Health is a complex system based on many subsystems that can fail. There is no single measure of health that we can track. If I had to pick a single indicator, it would be weight constancy.

Now, feeling good in your body seems right, but day to day, we often make small changes that have an impact over months, years, or even decades. It would be nice to be able to read early indications of whether an experiment or lifestyle change is successful or not. So, where exactly can we read markers of good health?

**Working memory.** I am primarily interested in mental performance. You can measure your IQ with online tests, however, you will get better at solving these tests over time. I find that I am not getting better a dual-N-back tests, which measure short-term memory and attention. There are mobile apps that you can download for free. Unfortunately, it takes 5 minutes to perform a single test. You'd need 3 rounds to get an accurate reading, and you would ideally want to do that multiple times a day.

**Meditation.** Meditation cultivates the mind. In addition, a clear mind that investigates itself and the body can examine whether mind and body are in a good shape. Look for mindfulness of the body (*kāyagatāsati*), for instance, as practiced by the Goenka Vipassana organization. The ability to direct the mind to perform the exercise is an indirect measurement of clarity of mind.

**Weight.** I monitor my weight. It seems to be fairly stable within a few hundred grams. A change in weight is probably a marker for a dramatic change in the body. Monitoring will allow me to detect this and decide whether or not to continue or backtrack on the current experiment.

**Inflammations, allergies.** Oftentimes, your body will give you early signs of a more serious condition in the form of inflammations and allergies. The connection to the underlying causes is difficult to see. Once you have reached a healthy state, however, a new inflammation is easy to track by inspecting changes in dietary habits or other factors over the past week or two.

**Continuous glucose monitors.** Used by diabetics,

## 3.4. GROOMING PHYSICAL HEALTH

continuous glucose monitors help you measure sugar levels in the blood stream. To date, the technology which is based on blood samples is the only reliable one. However, optical technology seems promising. Since it is used by diabetics, it requires medical certification and a prescription to purchase. That leads to slow progress.

**Blood tests.** Extended blood tests performed by companies such as inside tracker can be obtained. For various reasons I am not using them.

**Heart rate monitors.** Measuring your heart rate throughout the day, and throughout seasons tells you a little bit about caloric consumption of various activities. I wear a tracker in the form of a smart watch. I like to watch my heart rates mostly for entertainment purposes.

**EEG devices.** You can monitor your EEG signals during sleep. The classification of sleep in different phases is subjective with low inter-annotator agreement. Sleep phases from your watch tend to be inaccurate. I owned an EEG band for a couple of years but was never able to derive meaningful actionable intelligence.

**Urine strips.** There are urine strips which measure your ketones and other substances. They tend to be inaccurate. It is believed that your ketone levels in blood, once in a ketogenic state, return to a lower baseline. Therefore, the keto strips are only useful to track transitions. Urine is non-invasive but doesn't seem to have much useful signal.

**Microbiome and stool.** Part of the quantified self movement is focused on measuring your microbiome. After all, the digestive system produces more dopamine than your brain! Additionally, it possesses a highly diverse DNA. As the saying goes, a happy belly leads to a happy mind.

I am optimistic that this will become moderately useful in the next decade or so.

### 3.4.2 Sleep

Sleep has been a pet peeve of mine for many years. I have had terrible sleep for as long as I can remember. Rare is the night when I can sleep uninterrupted.

**Morning feel.** While it is tempting to evaluate good sleep on the basis of the sense of well-being when you wake up, I found that this correlates poorly with mental performance throughout the day.

**Polyphasic sleep.** You can read Chaucer and ancient texts in multiple languages, and you will find that there were times prior to the industrial revolution when people used to sleep in two tranches (biphasic sleep). Leonardo da Vinci was known to sleep for 20 minutes every 4 hours (polyphasic). I have tried multiple variants and none really worked for me.

**Alcohol.** Alcohol consumption will interfere with sleep. You may be less sensitive to it, but it's always a bad idea.

**Caffeine.** Caffeine will impair your sleep as well, more is always bad. You can use caffeine to conceal some of the effects of poor sleep, but, in an adapted state, the un-caffeinated state achieves better performance.

**Temperature.** It seems that a slightly cooler temperature might help. You can buy temperature regulation systems and experiment with the temperature profile over time.

**Stress.** Stress and anxiety will disrupt your sleep. Eliminate the causes for stress. Retirement helps, and so

## 3.4. GROOMING PHYSICAL HEALTH

does withdrawal from excessive social activities. Behave well: your conscience will torment you more than you realize.

**Meditation and breathing exercises.** If you have trouble getting to sleep, meditation, yoga nidra, and breathing exercises (web search for 7-4-8 breathing exercise) might help. They settle the mind.

**Schedule.** In retirement, I found that sleeping at a set hour and getting up as soon as I wake up works the best. It is also less painful than waking up with an alarm clock at a given hour. Your body tells you when it is ready.

### 3.4.3 Nutrition

The state of nutrition advice is perplexing. Is milk good or bad? Meat? Fat? Salt? You will find different answers, sometimes going back and forth over the years, and passionately debated. Academic publications don't appear to be able to definitively answer even the simplest questions.

My goal is to maximize mental acuity throughout the day. Better sleep should be a marker of better health. The body should be lean with no excess muscle except around the spine. I do not find joy in engaging in physical exercise or sports.

**Fasting.** Fasting may have some benefits. If you need to lose weight, it might work as a protocol to restrict calorie intake. However, if you don't want to lose weight, then it may slow your metabolism and reduce muscle mass. I have a daily fasting 16-hour window between 4PM and 8AM. A few times a year, I will water fast for three to five days. Fasting allows me to reduce the overhead associated with meals – preparation and digestion. I eat my main meal around 8AM to 9AM and the second meal around 4PM is a lot lighter. I do not eat or snack otherwise.

**Low carb.** On most days, I follow a low carb diet similar to keto. Specifically, I avoid consuming any food or beverage that contains added sugar. Additionally, I refrain from eating potatoes, rice, bread, and pasta. Instead, I primarily rely on protein and fat for energy, although I do not adhere to a strict measurement of intake. This minimizes food coma.

**Meat or no meat.** While meat does introduce some food coma, it is an efficient way to consume nutrients. Only nuts are denser. It is also easy to prepare. In America, approximately 12 billion animals are slaughtered for food every year, with three quarters of them being chickens. The meat industry is appalling, and the use of antibiotics is worrisome. Industrially grown plants also use chemicals. The widely cited China Study by Campbell suggests consuming whole plant foods to minimize cancer risks. It's a combination of what you can grow to like, prepare, and eat safely, ethically, and inexpensively.

**Alcohol.** There is a lot of culture associated with alcohol. Wine appreciation is a part of any Western educated adult, particularly in France and Italy. However, alcohol is essentially toxic at all doses.

**Supplements.** As an optimist, for years I have been trying one supplement after another. Occasionally, they do have an effect. It may be that you are lacking some vitamin or mineral temporarily. Probiotics cured me of a lifelong issue with poor digestion. However, aside from that, the impacts are subtle, and it's not clear that they are, on the

## 3.4.4 Body training

The goal here is to maintain a body that will allow us to move with grace and dignity for as long as possible.

**Yoga.** Yoga fulfills the requirements of developing strength, balance, and flexibility. Strength is necessary for protecting the spine and maintaining balance, but excess muscle will get stiff. The more muscle you develop, the more time you must dedicate to maintaining flexibility. Muscle development around the spine is crucial for maintaining an upright posture. Beyond that, it's not clear that developing limbs is necessary. Enhancing flexibility and strength will reduce the risk that you break something accidentally.

**Avoid low metabolic rate.** A higher metabolic rate appears to support mental activity. A higher state of energy prevents lethargy. Engaging in some amount of cardio exercise appears to be necessary for this purpose.

**Walking.** Walking is a relaxing activity. Daily walking outside will get you sun exposure, fresh air, and exercise your eyes. You can listen to audio-books while you walk to reclaim the time.

**Sports.** Like Churchill, who lived to 90 years old, I have done absolutely no sports since I left university. You can easily overdo it. I don't enjoy it. I started practicing yoga at a beginner level since retirement.

**Survival skills.** Considering your plans, you may need some survival skills, such as training for self-defense. Boat people and refugees had to swim sometimes days to get to their destination. If you are capable of running a marathon, you are in a pretty good shape.

**Don't do dumb things.** I am always astonished by the risks that many otherwise rational people are willing to take for a fleeting slightly pleasurable experience. Weigh the pros and cons when you are risking life and limbs.

**Don't overdo it.** There is a tendency, particularly among males, to over-exert. You might build excessive muscles that reduce your flexibility and overall health. Intense exercise can damage your spine or create an imbalance in posture.

### 3.4.5 Unexpected infirmity

You can adjust slowly to loss of vision and hearing. You would be surprised by how difficult life becomes if you suddenly lose the use of your dominant hand or sight, even temporarily. Simply dressing up can feel like an insurmountable task.

Unlike finance, the probability is actually small and actuarial tables should be accurate. Loss of limb is 0.5%.

| Age range | Blindness per capita |
|---|---|
| 16-64 | 2% |
| 65+ | 6.6% |

It's always good to be able to function somewhat without your dominant hand.

## 3.5 Mental health

Like our body, we should have a mind that is in good working condition. Generally speaking, we are looking at basic interventions to keep ourselves in a roughly happy state.

## 3.5. MENTAL HEALTH

### 3.5.1 Evaluation

Before we talk about basic maintenance, let's first explore how we can assess where we are or track progress. There are any number of psychological tests online that you can use.

**Pebbles.** Apparently, there is an exercise in Tibet. You take a heap of pebbles. Then, wait for thoughts to come into your mind. For each negative thought, put it on a pile to your left. For each positive thought, put it on the right. There is no need to judge or steer yourself to think positively. It's enough to recognize thoughts for what they are.

**Generosity.** Truly happy people are generous. Imagine you won the lottery. In these first five seconds, what are you thoughts? Throw a big party or build a world destroying rocket?

**Gratitude.** Similarly, a state of gratitude or feeling happy to be alive goes hand in hand with a happy mind.

**Energy or lethargy.** If you feel lethargic and lacking in motivation or energy, then you are generally less happy. Extended periods of dullness are a precursor to depression.

**Attitude towards the future.** If you are anxious about the future, rather than looking forward to it, then it's a sign that you are less happy.

**Enjoyment of food.** Food tends to taste bland when you're less happy.

These tests are better used as markers of progress, rather than a gauge of absolute health. A happy mind, like a healthy body, allows you to live your life more fully.

### 3.5.2 Intervention

How do you go about improving mental health? By and large, maintaining a healthy body is half the battle. Usually, maintaining energy will work.

**Sleep.** Sleeping well enough and long enough should improve your energy and mental well-being.

**Meditation.** Meditation will act as additional sleep and reduce stress. It also improves happiness levels in subtle ways.

**Reduce causes of stress.** Eliminating causes of stress, such as over-commitment, extra marital affairs, etc, also improves well-being.

**Social network.** Hanging out with friends can be a source of energy, in moderation. Too much of it and the emotional entanglement will be its own source of stress.

**Chemicals.** Some chemical substances act as stimulants, and modify the dopamine and serotonin pathways. It is better to do without them if possible, as they have some side effects and can be addictive.

**Other medical treatments.** There appears to be some progress with trans-cranial direct stimulation. This is a rather crude instrument, and its side-effects are unknown.

We will describe how to manage and develop happiness in the next chapter. This is meant to be basic maintenance.

## 3.6 Summary

In this chapter, we made a distinction between health and longevity. We cannot expect much of a life extension, so living healthy should be the primary goal. The body merely

## 3.6. SUMMARY

serves as a support for the mind. It should allow us to lead a dignified and independent existence, free from pain. It should also be fit enough to avert dangerous situations. When working well, it should support mental activity and enable us to enjoy sensual pleasures.

Our senses will deteriorate over time. The history of medical progress should leave us with some realistic expectations regarding potential advancements over the next half century. In practice, I wouldn't count on medical procedures that would restore mobility or sight, the most important faculties. So it's better to protect our precious body from permanent damage.

Surprisingly, there aren't many reliable easy ways to track how healthy we are. Testing working memory and monitoring weight stand out as crude, but easy and effective ways to measure how well we are doing. The biggest levers we have are sleep, nutrition, and exercise. Unfortunately, there is no one-size-fits-all protocol that works for everyone. You should try various routines and see which ones work for you. Finally, we have to be cognizant of the possibility that we might suddenly lose a limb or sight in a sudden accident. The probability is relatively small, so you may choose how to prepare accordingly.

We cover the basics of mental health. It's hard to tell if you are mentally healthy. If you have positive thoughts, feel lucky, generous, and energetic, you're doing well. To enhance your health, good sleep and meditation should be first on the list. Eliminate stress from your life and manage your social life carefully. If it is serious, medical intervention is in order.

On the whole, there isn't much you can do in the planning phase. You can certainly recognize if your current lifestyle is unhealthy, particularly regarding stress and sleep. When it comes to retirement, you have to understand that the upside is relatively limited. The best case is to have a body that doesn't get in the way of your enjoyment of life. Beyond that, none of these crunches and push-ups will help. You can't extend your life by much, and you can't expect the medical establishment to make serious progress in the next half century. It is for you to decide how much time and treasure you want to allocate to health. There's not much we know, there isn't much we know that works, and we can't really tell if it works for the most part.

If you plan to experience pleasure through the body – food, sex, runner's high, visual arts, music – then know that habituation, and the decay of the senses, will dampen your experience. There is one sense that you will preserve: the mind. And that is the topic for our next chapter.

## 3.7 Reading further

Before we proceed, I have to note that, to my chagrin, a number of famous authors in behavioral psychology are accused of fraud. You are free to form your own judgment on the matter. While some scientific articles have been retracted, no books were recalled: they are still available to buy as if nothing happened. Other books which base their work on their research have yet to be amended or withdrawn.

## 3.7. READING FURTHER

 **Altered Traits: Science Reveals How Meditation Changes Your Mind, Brain, and Body by Daniel Goleman, Richard Davidson.** A book about the triumphs of neuro-plasticity. Take with a grain of salt. This shows that deep changes in the brain can occur with and without chemical intervention.

 **Being Mortal: Medicine and What Matters in the End by Atul Gawande.** The books gives a history of medicine, and final patient care.

 **How to Change Your Mind: What the New Science of Psychedelics Teaches Us**

**About Consciousness, Dying, Addiction, Depression, and Transcendence by Michael Pollan.** This is a primer on the experimental use of controlled substances for various medical purposes. Some appear to induce behavioral changes that are eerily similar to religious experiences. Could you drug your way to enlightenment?

 **How Not to Die: Discover the Foods Scientifically Proven to Prevent and Reverse Disease by Michael Greger MD, Gene Stone.** Dr. Greger has a YouTube channel and can be quite entertaining. He's advocating a vegetarian diet. He has been accused of cherry-picking studies.

 **How We Die: Reflections on Life's Final Chapter by Sherwin B. Nuland.** This book shows what happens in the final years of our life, including long-term care.

## 3.7. READING FURTHER

 **Lifespan: Why We Age - and Why We Don't Have To by David A. Sinclair PhD, Matthew D. LaPlante.** David Sinclair is a somewhat controversial figure because of his association with hype and commercial ventures. He was associated with the claim that resveratrol (found in red wine) enhanced longevity. This does show the current state-of-the-art in longevity research.

 **Overdiagnosed: Making People Sick in Pursuit of Health by Dr. H. Gilbert Welch, Dr. Lisa M. Schwartz, Dr. Steven Woloshin.** As the title suggests, the medical establishment tends to recommend unnecessary intervention, which, on the whole, are a net negative. This is a **must-read**.

 **Sleep Smarter: 21 Essential Strategies to Sleep Your Way to a Better Body, Better Health, and Bigger Success by Shawn Stevenson.** Sleep is one the most important things you do, each and every day. Try to do it better.

 **The Emperor of All Maladies: A Biography of Cancer by Siddhartha Mukherjee.** The history of cancer research, from Galen onward. It's astounding how little we know, and how medical research relies on anthropomorphic analogies to design treatments. This is a **must-read**.

## 3.7. READING FURTHER

**Whole: Rethinking the Science of Nutrition by T. Colin Campbell PhD/PhD, Howard Jacobson.** This is by the author of the China study which correlates a low incidence of cancer with a plant-based diet. This is a good start if you want to reason yourself into a vegetarian diet.

# Chapter 4

# Purpose

Now that we've covered how to stay alive and away from indigence, let's see what it is that we're going to do in retirement. We've described it so far generically as a happy ever after, a life worth living. Let's find out how to build the overarching plan of what you're going to live for in the next half century.

## 4.1  In this chapter

Unlike finance and health, purpose relies on subjective experience. This does mean that there is no single right answer: it's really up to you. We can, however, provide a framework for rationally analyzing what our future prospects will be.

Firstly, we must whittle down the scope of what purpose should be. Ostensibly, there is a reflexive quality to it: the purpose is what you want to do, and you decide what you want to do. We'll question some culturally accepted trade-offs, notably, that our happiness runs counter to, and is subordinate to, the good of a community. We'll give some desirable traits that, when fulfilled, will lead to a goal that is highly likely to be worth pursuing.

Secondly, we turn to the Buddhist doctrine as a framework for establishing the goal. It offers solutions to well-known conundrums, such as the fickle nature of relying on material attainments. We recognize that the mind is our own to command, and that there is a process to nudging it through the scientific process of rational hypothesis formation and experimentation. You can use the language and framework of Buddhist psychology without adopting its assumptions. Lastly, following the Buddhist path entails risks: it may lead to false paths and, more frequently, giving up along the way (apostasy).

## 4.2 Goal design

The functional goal of finding purpose in retirement is to keep us satisfied and fulfilled for half a century. It is simply good enough to avoid failure: being disaffected enough to willfully terminate that arrangement.

To that end, we must find **purpose** in life, that happy ever after. It lies somewhere between finding true meaning in life and being just comfortable enough to shirk work. We shoot for the highest while designing the goal. During the execution phase, we pick what is attainable. In that sense, it is no different from financial planning.

As with **finance**, there are many books on the topic in self-improvement and religion, and many of them provide reasonable tools to approximate what is appropriate

## 4.2. GOAL DESIGN

to each individual. For that advice to stick, however, we must thoroughly understand and internalize the reasoning process behind it. We've covered mental health in the previous chapter – tactical advice for managing day to day mental wellness – this is strategic thinking. Because it is a complex topic, let's first narrow down the notion of what we are trying to achieve.

### 4.2.1 Confounding factors

**Non disputandum gustandum.** A physicist and a mathematician are challenged to design the largest enclosure with the least amount of material. After a few calculations, the physicist determines that a circular shape will encompass the largest amount of land. The mathematician wraps a fence around himself and declares: "I am outside".

There's a lot of confusion about happiness. Let's poke at different points to gradually open our mind away from preconceived notions.

**Singing in the shower.** First, happiness is sometimes equated to pleasure. Pleasure, in turn, can be fleeting or lasting. Without defining happiness precisely, we would posit that we choose a lasting state of well-being against the temporary bliss of a heroin fix. Imagine, if you will, that mental state when you wake up, well-rested and full of energy, looking forward to the day knowing that it's going to be a good day, smiling to yourself.

**Sitting quietly in a room alone.** While we made great strides in modern philosophy, most people in the

West have resigned themselves to a reality where the pursuit of meaning in life is inconclusive. Consequently, they completely give up on mental development and instead focus in external factors, such as wealth. All the while, however, they tend to feel a profound lack that manifests as a general unease that they cannot pin down. They attempt to wash it over by distracting themselves. People often the search for meaning because they are confused about what they are looking for. We *can* take steps towards lifting the veil.

**It's a matter of preference.** Unlike finance, where total net worth in liquid assets is an inter-subjective measure of success, purpose, and the achievement thereof, is subjective. No one else can observe what is in your mind. It is your prerogative to decide what is best.

> **Musical apostasy.** So satisfied was Carl Orff with the success of Carmina Burana, he wrote to his publisher: "Everything I have written to date, and which you have, unfortunately, published, can be destroyed. With Carmina Burana my collected works begin." When you change your mind, does it negate the good intentions that you had previously? Does the happiness that you experienced vanish as its memory becomes tainted?

**It can change over time.** There is no known rigorous definition of what defines a life well-lived. Our views and system of values can change, sometimes dramatically so. Reversals of opinions, overwhelmingly on the side of regret, routinely occur on death beds.

## 4.2. GOAL DESIGN

**It is not for you to decide.** Unfortunately, you cannot simply decree that you will be happy. Your mind decides *if* you're happy, and for most people, you will be aware of that, but you can't decide to be happy by fiat of reason. Wise preparation includes setting rational goals and corralling the mind towards a beneficial end.

**The Saint and the Hedonist.** Oftentimes, it is believed that there are opposing goals in life: sacrificing one's life for society and enjoying the dissolute life of a profligate. We will see that it is a false dichotomy. Mortifying oneself constantly will lead to a miserable life and wasting away one's time in drunken stupor will inevitably lead to regret. A truly happy person is spontaneously generous and a truly generous person is spontaneously happy.

**It is a composite objective.** When searching for a goal, keep in mind that multiple factors come into play. The solution could be a combination of factors or a goal subject to some constraints. For example, you may want to establish your reputation in some field of endeavor, but without sacrificing ethical values. It would be good to reflect on the importance of each factor to you.

**Purpose and happiness.** Purpose and happiness are intimately linked. As a goal, purpose should be happiness. Conversely, living a meaningful life with purpose confers happiness.

Now that we're starting to understand how to set the objective, we need to answer two epistemological questions. Firstly, since we our hearts and minds change, how do we know that we have set the correct goal? Second, if the goal is met, what does success look like?

## 4.2.2 A life worth living

We're aiming at making as rational a decision as we can. First, we may change our goals during life. Is there any point in time which has the utmost importance? Should we consider happiness over time, encompassing all moments in life? Or does the act of forgetting and a change in values invalidate previous happiness (or misery)?

Let's work through a few scenarios.

> **Youth is wasted on the young.** There may come a time, in your old age, when you wish you could just once more slip into your mind and body of your yesteryears, when tying your shoes and going to the toilet seemed so easy. There's a time and place for certain enjoyments. Minimize regrets.

> **Pascal's wager: epilogue.** In Pascal's time, mathematicians were employed by the aristocracy to gain an edge at the gambling table, like quantitative hedge funds do today. Pascal's wager rests on the idea that if there is any chance of infinite gains in the after life, then you should take that chance. He must have found more to life than a rational bet. While not entirely reverting to a dissolute existence, he did reverse himself. His own illness and his sister's death might have shaken him. He pronounced that "sickness is the natural state of Christians". Then, on his deathbed: "May God never abandon me". It's hard to keep a bet on the unobservable.

## 4.2. GOAL DESIGN

**Deathbed apostasy.** There's nothing that focuses the mind better than the prospect of imminent death. From a rational point of view, the final moment is the point when we have 100% hindsight, and it is where all experience can be integrated. Many people regret past actions and life choices. We should endeavor to act and behave in such a way that, when the time comes, we can look upon our life with pride and satisfaction. In the words of Warren Buffett, find out what you want to have written on your tombstone and live by it.

> **Now is not the time to make new enemies.** On his deathbed, Voltaire was exhorted to renounce the Devil. Wisely, he refused. Death is the end of the observable world. What follows could be nothing, eternity, or anything in between. We just don't know. The consequences of your actions in this life could be unbounded.

**In the name of the unobservable after-life.** The deathbed is also a favorite venue for religions to proselytize. It is possible that there would be a continuation after death. In fact, it could be eternal and, according to Pascal's wager, infinitely more important than an entire life. However, if you have multiple choices of religions with opposing views, the objective function is not calculable. For instance, if two opposing religions say that you must convert at once or face eternal hell, then you have no rational bet other than picking one (unless you are allowed to change your mind). We have to use our judgment to assess the possibility that the religious views are wrongly interpreted, or simply wrong. Bombing a crowded subway does not seem to be a likely behavior that would be sanctioned by most religions if interpreted correctly. Be kind to your neighbors seems like it would fit any plausible religious doctrine.

> **Post partum.** Before anesthesia was introduced in Britain in the nineteenth century, surgeries were a painful affair. In China, mushrooms were given to forget about the pain. If you forgot about it, does it matter if it really happened?

**Forgetting.** "Nothing is impossible... for the man who doesn't have to do it himself". Another objection is that early pains and sacrifices in life are forgotten after a decade. If we constantly shoot for results a decade or more away, we may delay gratification until our few last breaths. Therefore, while formulating our epitaph rationally, we should take care to consider ourselves as an important participant whose wants and needs are weighted in. Self sacrifice is also hard to implement.

**Adaptation.** Another line of argument posits that the future is uncertain and it is futile to forecast so far in advance. Our opinions are shaped by lived experience, and there is a fair amount of adaptation to our current situation that can change our goals significantly. We should continually update our views and prospects for the future. However, we can steer the ship meaningfully, and some values are unlikely to be substantially wrong.

While setting goals, we are faced with a false dichotomy: enjoying a glass a wine now versus a hangover later. We can look for a goal that is pleasant to execute today and worthwhile in retrospect. Generally speaking, we want to be able to lie on our deathbed, reflecting on a pleasant, happy life, and, possibly, a like after-life, thinking, "this was a life worth living, and what a wonderful journey it was". It's the journey and the destination.

### 4.2.3 Success is happiness

Sometimes you'll hear that there is a tension between success and happiness. By success, one usually means material, religious, or ethical goals being met. By happiness, one usually means pleasure or ethical fulfillment. In simpler terms, reason and emotion are often viewed as conflicting with each other.

Let's review the different possibilities. We will stylize the situations where it's all or nothing, but in reality, there is a continuum.

| Scenario | Reason | Emotion |
|---|---|---|
| Heroin addict | No | No |
| Marilyn Monroe | Yes | No |
| A modest fisherman | No? | Yes |
| Dalai Lama | Yes | Yes |

**Losing control.** First, a heroin addict has lost control of their life in a way that makes them miserable and unhappy with how things turned out. It is an undesirable outcome on both ends. Addiction of any kind tends to have a similar outcome with varying degrees. Loss of mental control during fits of rage, for instance, is in the same category.

**Successful and depressed.** Look anywhere and you'll

find that some of the most accomplished figures in their field of endeavor are spectacularly unhappy. Sometimes there were pre-conditions, but mostly a different path in life might have resulted in not causing depression, or finding a cure for depression. Imagine yourself, gun in hand, destitute, unloved and alone in your living room, having donated your entire fortune to a charity benefiting ungrateful people, you sit there contemplating the final exit. Was it all worth it? We have the most control over ourselves: we should be suspicious of goals that involve making others happy when you cannot make yourself happy.

**Happy and living small.** Now put the case of a modest fisherman. He goes through the trials and tribulations of life with modest expectations, and low stress. Socio-economically, reputationally, and otherwise, he is a most unremarkable man. He lacks the drive and ambition to strive for more, and is relatively content, or some would say resigned, with his lot. His condition, and indeed himself, is contemned by the large majority of society. He is not "successful" in the modern colloquial sense, but he achieves success in the true sense of fulfilling the goals that he set for himself.

**High performer and happy.** Let's now consider a famous person, perhaps the Dalai Lama or Warren Buffett. They are high achievers in their respective fields and they look reasonably happy. It is hard to gauge whether a person is truly happy, but let us presume that they are. It is possible to be both successful and live a happy existence. When setting our goal, if we choose to deviate from this ideal, there must be a good reason. It could be that, as in the previous case, we choose to value our own lived

## 4.2. GOAL DESIGN

experience less than some other objective, or, as a tactical compromise, we perceive that we cannot achieve both.

We have seen that success is contingent on defining a goal. Success means meeting that goal. That goal must be achievable. All other objectives (*e. g.* money, fame) are subordinated within that objective. If the goal is met, we are happy with the result. If the goal is not met, we are unhappy with the result. Therefore, being satisfied with, or happy with the result is a byword for success. We have some latitude in selecting the goal, but it something that we have to be truly content with. We should also choose a worthwhile goal that is free from hardship. Not meeting the goal leads to unhappiness, so the bar should be modest.

### 4.2.4 Desirable properties

> **The government we deserve.** Thomas Sowell: "The fact that so many successful politicians are such shameless liars is not only a reflection on them, it is also a reflection on us. When the people want the impossible, only liars can satisfy". Don't set your expectations too high lest you be fooled. Is it possible to fulfill all promises, or is it a scam?

So far, we've left the question of the specific goal in mind fairly open. It seems that being the undisputed world champion in World of Warcraft will work as well as curing malaria. Here, we lay more specific properties of a worthy goal. For each, we posit that, *ceteris paribus*, it's better to design a goal with than without these properties. That will help prioritize some goals over others.

Before we proceed, however, we must first note that there is no claim that these properties form a complete set. You can add your own properties. They are part of my own design requirements. You will find that they are known technical concepts in Buddhism. You are welcome to use them or disregard their utility as you see fit.

We'll go through each item on the list:

- Sustainable and stable

- Unconditioned

- Good for self and others simultaneously

- Attainable with continuous improvement

- The ultimate goal

> **When money is not the end.** When asked about how much money he thought was enough, John D. Rockefeller, one of the most successful industrialists the world has ever seen, famously replied: "Just a little bit more". His goal was not money, but accumulating money. You could do that forever.

**Sustainable and stable.** We're going to spend half a century in retirement. Some, perhaps all of that time will be spent in pursuit of a goal, and some in basking in success. It is vital that we pick a goal that we can pursue for decades, and not burn out. Furthermore, the goal has to be worthy enough for us not to change our mind. Finally,

## 4.2. GOAL DESIGN

the final state must be stable: we could, say, aim to become the world's richest person, but once we attain that position, we would have to look for something else.

**Unconditioned.** Some objectives are easier to attain. The less they require to reach and maintain, the better. If you set your mind to building a homemade nuclear reactor, then, well, you'll need to collect a lot of prerequisites. To operate it lawfully would necessitate constant upkeep. That's an easier goal than most of us set! We want to keep ourselves happy, that is, satisfy that insatiable mind of ours. We set unbounded goals that require unbounded conditions to be met.

**Good for self and others.** Let's say we want a certain goal for ourselves. It's better to be able to achieve this goal while benefiting others as well. For instance, getting rich is great, but we should choose producing a good that helps others and selling it at a reasonable price as opposed to outright stealing the money. Similarly, would you kill someone for, say, giving underprivileged children a better education? Then why should you choose to forfeit your existence over it? There is a class of goals that make you happier as you make others happier.

**Dorothy Parker.** Some things we can never attain.

Four be the things I am wiser to know:
Idleness, sorrow, a friend, and a foe.

Four be the things I'd been better without:
Love, curiosity, freckles, and doubt.

Three be the things I shall never attain:
Envy, content, and sufficient champagne.

Three be the things I shall have till I die:
Laughter and hope and a sock in the eye.

**Attainable with continuous improvement.** Say you'd like to prove Fermat's theorem in no more than 5 pages. It's a risky proposition. You may spend your entire life and have nothing to show for it. Many religions and ascetic practices have a similar payoff curve. We would prefer to have a continuous improvement. First, it helps to keep track of progress, as long as the goal is measurable. Second, if we terminate prematurely, we will still have achieved whatever we have done so far. Furthermore, it is called "convexity" in optimization theory. If there is a reachable maximum (versus just improving to infinity), then improving little by little will eventually reach the maximum. Second, the maximum is unique. However we reach it, there's no ambiguity as to what is best.

**Consequences of being both stable and attainable with continuous improvement.** So, let's imagine you have reached your maximum: what you have and what you want are the same. If what you want is stable, it has that element of bliss – the feeling that nothing needs to be added or subtracted. The ultimate bliss is an intense sense

## 4.2. GOAL DESIGN

of satisfaction. It is free of – devoid of – desire.

> **Use your time well.**
> But wherefore do not you a mightier way
> Make war on this blood Tyrant, Time?
> And fortify yourself in your decay
> With means more blessed than my barren rhyme?
> Now stand you on the top of happy hours,
> With many maiden gardens, yet unset,
> With virtuous wish would bear your living flowers,
> Much liker than your painted counterfeit.
> So should the lines of life that life repair
> Which this, Time's pencil or my pupil pen,
> Neither in inward worth nor outward fair
> Could make you live your self in eyes of men.
> To give away yourself, keeps yourself still,
> And you must live, drawn by your own sweet skill.

Shakespeare wrote a series of Elizabethan-style sonnets about procreation. The identity of the recipient was never confirmed. In this one, he urges his reader to consider the advance of time as a forcing function, and argues that offspring is better than writing.

**The ultimate goal.** If you have collected a list of potential goals, then you can probably rank them. For instance, being rich, being the richest man in the world, being the richest man that ever lived, can be ranked numerically according to calculated wealth. If you want to maximize your chances of success, then you want to pick the lowest net worth. However, the goal might not be stable, because you might sooner adjust your target to a new net worth as soon as you get close. If you set your goal to "getting as rich as I can", as John D. Rockefeller did, you could be continuously improving, but your search does not admit a maximum and has no bounds. To be satisfactory, you have to shoot high enough in your hierarchy of goals so that you maximize your end result. At a minimum, the goal should be better than your corporate job.

## 4.3 Buddhism

I will be using the framework of Buddhism extensively for the rest of the discussion. While a religious framework may be off-putting to many, as it was for me initially, there is a great deal of rational argument and realism about human psychology that can be found in Buddhism. If you are spiritually inclined, it also promises that supra-mundane attainment is possible (though difficult) during your lifetime.

It is not my place to explain or endorse the whole Buddhist world. We will only use what we need. Again, each concept can be questioned, accepted or rejected, and has likely a considerable history and body of literature devoted to its clarification. We will give the terms in the original Pali language so that they can be researched. Unfortunately, many of those terms do not have a universally accepted English translation, so searching using a particular translation will lead to biased results. We provide them in our own understanding. The Buddhist canon contains a large portion of teachings of the Buddhist throughout his career, and as such, is designed to be understood by a large audience; they are readable without the aid of (the vast)

## 4.3. BUDDHISM

commentary.

### 4.3.1 Enthymemes

In rhetoric, enthymemes are axioms that are not explicitly stated. We have already seen that they are problematic: the dichotomy between success and happiness, and one's well-being versus others. The Buddhist doctrine states that there are universal laws governing the subjective (mental) experience. In Newtonian physics, we can all agree that one person can throw a rock in the air to validate the theory, and the results, if observed by multiple trustworthy people, will satisfy our requirement for truth. With subjective experience, however, everyone has to do their own work of validating the laws, verifying each hypothesis one by one for oneself.

We'll revisit the desirable properties and restate them within the context of Buddhist doctrine. Many of them break pernicious enthymemes that are part of our culture.

**Sustainable and stable.** The anti-thesis of ultimate stability is impermanence and uncertainty (*anicca*). The premise is that what arises will eventually cease. So, if you tie up happiness with a material possession or mental state, you will not be able to maintain it forever. Therefore, parting with, or actively maintaining that possession is a source of anxiety. There are gradations in durability and defensibility: diamonds are quite durable, and, say, the memory of a past achievement will stay with you until you can no longer remember it, die, or it is supplanted.

**Unconditioned.** If happiness is predicated on certain conditions being met, then it can be displaced. Conditions that are hard to set up and maintain make happiness more difficult to achieve and sustain. In the extreme, happiness that has no conditions (*asaṅkhata*) is the best. If you need special equipment (yes, that Ferrari), a healthy body, a sharp intellect, then know what you are getting into. If there is happiness that's available anytime, anywhere, on tap, as it were, it would be the ideal goal.

**Puritanism: the haunting fear that somebody, somewhere, may be happy.** The values of hard work and doing your duty above all else created the prosperity of the United States. Today, the culture seems to be focused on happiness only, while indulgence feeling shameful at the same time. Perhaps there is a better way.

**Good for self and others simultaneously: a win-win.** Deep in the cultural consciousness lies a notion that one has to sacrifice oneself, and the pursuance of one's benefit is somewhat amoral. Religion, society at large, one's spouse and family stand on the opposite side. In Buddhism, there is a win-win solution: *attāaṁ rakkhanto paraṁ rakkhati, paraṁ rakkhanto attānaṁ rakkhati* (protecting yourself, you protect others; protecting others, you protect yourself). There is a recognition that there is a happiness arising from helping, or at least not harming others. It's an easier day when you interact with people with kindness and get kindness in return. **Observable.** Known as *ehipassiko*, "Come and see," this concept means that results are observable. To a large extent, Buddhist assertions

## 4.3. BUDDHISM

are falsifiable (can be proven wrong) and verifiable (validated). For instance, the concept of *anavajjasukha*, that joy arises from living a blameless life (not hurting others), can be evaluated rationally and through introspection. The existence of deities and unobservable spirits cannot be ascertained definitively one way or another.

**Attainable.** One of the key aspects of religion is to bring transcendence to mundane life. The idea is that we fail to find meaning in the mundane, so we place it in the supra-mundane. Therefore, it is not achievable during your lifetime. The Buddhist doctrine asserts that not only worldly benefits can be observed along the way, enlightenment can be achieved during one's lifetime, oftentimes translated as here and now (*sandiṭṭhiko*).

**Continuous improvement.** In our culture, there is an assumption that pain is necessary to obtain the ultimate gain. There are various strands of self-mortification and ascetic practitioners that sacrificing pleasure in the current life is the price to pay for a comfortable after-life. In the extreme, we can find suicide bombers in that category. The Buddhist doctrine posits that there are benefits to be had all throughout the journey. It is translated as good in the beginning, good in the middle, and good in the end (*ādikalyāṇaṁ majjhekalyāṇaṁ pariyosānakalyāṇaṁ*). If, for whatever reason, you abort the development, you will still have made some forward progress along the way. You get partial credit.

**The ultimate goal.** Previous considerations notwithstanding, you should pick the goal that has the most value. This is a hard one to assess. For the sake of retirement, the low bar is to be better than the *status quo* of full-time employment. Like any decision in directing your life, clarify your reasoning for the various candidates, be realistic about what you can achieve, and try to follow the logic to its conclusion. The idea of a gradual slide towards unassailable bliss doesn't sound so bad to me.

### 4.3.2 Process

You may have been convinced to reach the final Buddhist goal, or at least make some efforts towards developing your mind towards that direction. This is how to progress towards the goal.

The Buddhist doctrine is like a map. It shows you the way to the final destination, but you must follow the path yourself, and verify against landmarks to see if you progressed in the right direction, and check whether the map itself is accurate, and that you know where you are.

You progress step by step, shedding light on further truths as you go:

1. **Reason**: you can use your mental reasoning ability to assess what the next steps are. Perhaps you are intrigued by the points made in this book or elsewhere. Examine whether the theory is plausible and holds up to logical scrutiny. Say you consider being kind as a universal principle to be followed. Does this really work in the long term? Under what conditions will this lead to more happiness?

2. **Make a leap of faith**: you develop the confidence to test a hypothesis. You run the experiment, let's say, try kindness instead of stern reprimand in the

face of someone making a mistake. You need to have enough faith, acquired by reasoning through the possible scenarios, that this could be a potentially better response. If this works, you will gain more confidence the next time to try again. As a society, we have spent billions verifying some of Einstein's theories. We looked through the math, looked at the movement of planets, and it checked out. As more and more falsifiable predictions matched, we developed more faith in the explanatory power of his theory.

3. **Monitor**: while there are some external consequences, the work in Buddhism is about transforming the mind. It is easier to control the mind than to control external conditions. For that, you need to keep an eye on the workings of the mind as they develop. This does not come naturally. In popular culture, this is called *mindfulness*. You have to monitor your reactions and lift the veil over the causal chain of events. For instance, anger does not arise out of the blue. It is a process starting with irritation, habits formed over the years, the thinking mind losing sight of the bigger picture, etc. If you are aware that anger is forming, you have a choice to stop it.

4. **Verify**: once you've run the experiment, say, you've reacted with kindness instead of anger. Did this have the desired effect? Did you gain a quantum of happiness? Are you calmer, experiencing less fear and agitation, and more peaceful as a result? Would you change something in the manner you ran the experiment the next time around? Learn from failed ex-

periments as well.

5. **Iterate**: hopefully, after a few experiments, you'll notice some positive change. Keep that new skill under your belt and find another hypothesis to try.

The teachings of the Buddha are vast and repetitive, sometimes excruciatingly detailed, and yet oddly vague on specifics. There is no right entry point or linear course to follow. Therefore, it's sometimes hard to know where to start. There are three domains of action:

1. **Ethical conduct (sīla)**: how you comport yourself, essentially, the various skillful ways of not hurting yourself and others.

2. **Collectedness (samadhi)**: this is also translated as stillness or concentration. This has to do with observing your mind inclining towards peace, away from agitation (fear, anger, desire, etc). Meditation is a way to set up a controlled environment where a lot of that work can be done.

3. **Wisdom (pañña)**: internalization and intelligent understanding of the doctrine. Reasoning, memorizing salient points of the doctrine, and a skill for tactful application of the principles go in that bucket.

Buddhism involves a process of developing the mind. You can memorize the tenets, and apply rules rigorously, but quick progress is not guaranteed. But, however much progress you make, I think it will be a life worth living.

## 4.3.3 Dangers

So, if you're so sure about this, why are you not a monk, you ask?

Well, because it might not stick. Here are the main issues that you can encounter:

- **Mis-interpretations**: the Buddha had a sense of humor, and the teaching material are full of word plays, imagery, and overloading a term with a more exalted meaning. Sometimes these differences in interpretation can lead to drastically different perspectives. For instance, the path is said to be *ekagagatā*, which can mean direct, one-pointed, or unified. Which translation you settle on has a direct consequence on how you develop focus and concentration during meditation.

- **Gurus**: the indiscriminate use of an intermediary to digest the vast teachings is directly frowned upon. First, because understanding the teachings for oneself through direct experience, internalizing them, is part of the transformation of the mind. Second, because gurus are human beings that have failings like any other beings, however eloquent and persuasive they can be. Overall, the Pali canon (to the exclusion of most of the commentary) is eminently approachable, and the risk of being led astray by a guru is comparatively high.

- **Slow progress**: breaking habits of the mind is an excruciatingly slow process. So slow, in fact, that it can take months or years to discern improvements.

What's worse, while the monitoring faculty is not fully developed, it can really feel like no progress has been made. While good deliberate action always has good results, the results might not manifest in the category or magnitude we expect. Because progress is hard to discern, it's hard to say what works best or credit any improvement to a specific behavior.

- **Shooting too high**: many people set the bar high early on. It's going to be enlightenment in 7 days. This leads almost inevitably to disappointment. Remembering that the path is gradual, we should be looking for fruits of the practice along the way: they are a good encouragement and serve as landmarks that the path goes in the right direction.

- **Trying too hard**: another path to disappointment is to try too hard to get results quickly. The Buddhist doctrine calls for diligence and instilling a sense of urgency, but this has to be balanced against striving too hard. The path of the ascetics leads to discomfort and strain, which prevent progress.

- **Trying too little**: lack of diligence will make it harder to discern progress and ensure you are on the right path. It's like a leaky bucket: progress made is quickly dissipated. The faster you progress, the happier you will be; you'll be coming back for more. Apply yourself with gentle resolve.

So, keep monitoring progress, be wary of misunderstandings, and be firm but patient.

## 4.4 Summary

It's been quite a dense chapter! Well worth the trouble for discovering the meaning of life, I say. Let's go through our thought process once again.

First, living a life worth living is a healthy purpose. If you want a mission statement, think about what you would want to be written on your tombstone, when you have maximum retrospective. We've found that there is no success without happiness and there is no happiness if we succeed in something we don't want. Therefore, success is synonymous with happiness. Happiness is a mental phenomenon. We've disassociated reason and emotion, and recognized that we have to slowly incline the mind towards our goal. We can use reason to design our goal by setting up requirements: the goal should be attainable; progress should be gradual and observable; the goal should have a minimal set of exogenous dependencies; the search and attainment should be sustainable and stable; there should be a win-win for ourselves and others; there should be no higher purpose fitting the same criteria.

Second, we've used the vocabulary of the Buddhist doctrine which gives a set of practical tools to deal with the mind. The doctrine shatters cultural trade-offs to achieve the goal requirements. In contrast to many philosophies, the Buddhist teachings are concerned with providing a set of tools for achieving your goal. The goal does not have to match the Buddhist ideal, but the tools will work best if they meet the requirements we have set. There is a process to follow: start with a rational inquiry; acquire the confidence to run an experiment; monitor progress; validate your findings against the initial hypothesis at the conclusion of the experiment; iterate until the goal is reached or you die. The process is no guarantee for success. The risk factors are: mis-understanding, too much faith, slow progress, over-estimating oneself, and lack of diligence.

The Buddhist doctrine states that if you apply yourself diligently and correctly, you can reach the ultimate goal in as little as seven days. I fully expect to spend the rest of my life without completing the Buddhist ultimate goal. However, the progress I will have made along the way will suffice to proclaim that it was a life well lived.

**A happiness that is out of this world.** Ajahn Chah (Luong Por Chah) was one of Thailand's most famous monks of the twentieth century. There is picture where he is shown mimicking a statue whose caption read: "Joy at last, to know that there is no happiness in this world." We look for happiness in this world in so many ways: cars, food, relationships. It never satiates. The freedom to know it's not there is liberating.

## 4.5 Reading further

**The Final Exit by Derek Humphry.** This is a book about "self-deliverance." Most people will be uncomfortable with the topic. The book was written by Derek Humphry, who, for ethical reasons, refused to share his experience in assisting with his sister's suicide. One person whom he refused to help, a quadriplegic, went forward anyway the best he could and set his apartment on fire. The book offers more humane ways. It's better to prepare a humane escape in case you ever need one, should you choose to use it or not when the time comes. This is a **must-read**.

**If You're so Smart, Why Aren't You Happy? by Raj Raghunathan.** Perhaps the best part of the book is its title. Think about it and look around. Why are so many talented people not devoting a second to reasoning about their own happiness?

 **Going Solo: The Extraordinary Rise and Surprising Appeal of Living Alone by Eric Klinenberg.** This book de-stigmatizes the path of celibacy. Today, you will see older people choose that path. They may be onto something.

 **Half the Sky: Turning Oppression into Opportunity for Women Worldwide by Nicholas D. Kristof, Sheryl WuDunn.** While this is a book about women, it contains a lot of information about the difficulty of abolishing human trafficking today. I found the anecdote about saving a woman from brothels particularly informative. This book lays everything plainly and the reality can be hard to read. This is a **must-read**, if you have the stomach, and if your charity donations go towards human trafficking.

## 4.5. READING FURTHER

 **Evidence of the Afterlife: The Science of Near-Death Experiences by Jeffrey Long, Paul Perry.** In the 1960s, cardiopulmonary resuscitation (CPR) was invented. Suddenly, many more people came back from the abyss. That lead to a flurry of books on the topic. This book shows that there is a commonality of experience, mystical or physical. Interestingly, there is much in common with deep meditative experiences, including a permanent change in attitude towards life's ultimate purpose. Some drugs can have similar results. This reinforces my belief that supra-mundane experience can occur in this life.

 **Mindfulness in Plain English by Bhante Henepola Gunaratana.** In my mind, one of the finest introductions to Buddhist mindfulness. He writes in the modern vernacular, but his exposition is quite faithful to the original doctrine. Additionally, he has au-

thored a few introductory books on Buddhism. They are all **must-reads**.

 **Stumbling on Happiness by Daniel Gilbert.** The book says it all: instead of explicitly optimizing for happiness, we instead pursue what we believe to be either symptoms or pre-requisites of happiness, without defining it. Sometimes we stumble on it. Don't rely on luck.

 **The Architecture of Happiness by Alain de Botton.** Entertaining as always, Alain de Botton looks at the Western tradition of happiness enunciated by Proust.

## 4.5. READING FURTHER

**The Blue Zones of Happiness: Lessons from the World's Happiest People by Dan Buettner, Ed Diener.** This book is another more methodical study of happiness. It studies places where people are happiest and seeks to identify common factors.

**The Happiness Hypothesis: Finding Modern Truth in Ancient Wisdom by Jonathan Haidt.** Can withdrawal from sensual pleasures make us happy? Jonathan Haidt pits the Stoics and Buddhists against the hedonists. He finds that the answer lies in-between. Unfortunately, he has but a partial understanding of Buddhism.

 **The Middle Length Discourses of the Buddha: A Translation of the Majjhima Nikaya by Bhikkhu Nanamoli, Bhikkhu Bodhi.** Bhikku Bodhi is the pre-eminent translator of his day. The Middle Length discourses offers the most comprehensive exposition of the Buddhist doctrine with the right level of detail. If you want to study Buddhism, it's a **must-read**. Don't skip Bhikkhu Bodhi's synopsis.

 **Satipatthana Meditation: A Practice Guide by Bhikkhu Analyo.** Written by a leading Buddhist scholar, this book is a kind of compendium of meditation practices that form the Satipatthana. You can find free audio and PDF versions online. It is a kind of modern and practical version of the Visuddhimagga.

## 4.5. READING FURTHER

**The Mind Illuminated: A Complete Meditation Guide Integrating Buddhist Wisdom and Brain Science for Greater Mindfulness by John Yates, Matthew Immergut and Jeremy Graves** The late Dr. John Yates, who went by Culadasa, had a background in physiology and neuroscience. He gives the clearest account of the various stages of meditation.

**When Breath Becomes Air by Paul Kalanithi.** There is no better time to reflect on the meaning of life then your ultimate breath. This is a story of a neurosurgeon dying of cancer grasping for purpose.

 **Opening the Door of Your Heart: And Other Buddhist Tales of Happiness by Ajahn Brahm.** A collection of anecdotes and stories that illustrate abstract notions of Buddhist doctrines. I'd recommend watching his talks on YouTube on the Buddhist Society of Western Australia, which has the same content and he is an engaging speaker. If you prefer reading, this is a **must-read**.

 **Irreducible Mind: Toward a Psychology for the 21st Century by Edward Kelly and Emily Williams Kelly.** This book curses the time when John B. (James) Watson, father of modern psychology, turned psychology into a science. Anything that wasn't readily observable was dismissed. The authors revisit the theories and areas of research that were left defunct. The explanation for genius, near-death experiences, hypnotism (then known as mesmerism), mind-brain filter theory, and

## 4.5. READING FURTHER

more. What we couldn't measure, we pretended didn't exist. This is a **must-read** (but voluminous).

# Chapter 5

# My Master Plan

Most books yield to the overwhelming desire for easy-to-follow advice. Instead, this book gives a mental framework to apply to your own situation. You may be busy, but if you're going to take a momentous decision that will shape the next few decades of your life, then I think it's fair that you devote a modicum of mental effort on it. There can be bad outcomes, but you want to be assured that you made a good decision.

I hope that you found various points of disagreement in my approach. You understand that I may have made mistakes or oversimplified. It's a sign that you are starting to apply the tools.

That said, I'd like to show you my own master plan. It will serve to fix ideas and as a starting point for your own plan. Like the rest of book, I am thinking in three facets: finance, health, and purpose. Let's get started.

## 5.1 Finance

There are four regimes when it comes to finance. Before retirement, you concentrate wealth. Then, most of the time in retirement will be just cruising along with the buffer strategy. At some point, this smooth sailing will be interrupted by a special event that may require radical changes. Finally, you may die with money left over.

### 5.1.1 Accumulation phase

It's relatively easy: save, save, and save some more until you have enough money to retire. I estimated that I needed approximately $3M. You'll see how this number was calculated in the next section. It's tempting to try to rush by implementing extreme saving measures, but you shouldn't.

**Value money.** I estimated my spending rate during retirement to be 3%. So, roughly speaking, 30 dollars saved is one dollar spent per annum in perpetuity. That gives you an idea how much you should value money today. A twice-daily $6 bubble tea fix will set you back $131k. Don't kill yourself to save quickly.

**Don't do anything you will regret.** Cheating your way to the goal is not worth it. Act in haste, repent at leisure. Some things you can never wipe clean.

**Overshoot by 10%.** Because the market may easily go up and down by 10% any given year, overshoot a little. I ended up retiring without an extra margin, right before the covid-19 market crash of 2020. Ouch.

**Engage in risky behavior.** During that period, you possess marketable skills and good cash flow. This is the

## 5.1. FINANCE

time to embark on high-reward, risky financial decisions. You will also learn from mistakes.

**You will get promoted.** Three or four times in my life, I was promoted meaningfully. Each time, except for the last one, two years in my new position would have doubled my entire net worth. My earning potential grew much faster than my return on financial assets.

***Carpe diem* rule.** Every so often, I spent 3% of my total net worth, in pure hedonistic consumption. You may die before you get to retire. A 3% will set you back approximately one year. Do it every five years for 20 years, you will have to work an additional five years. Much less, in practice, since you will save the most at the end.

> **And of calm mind, all passions spent.**
> In the same volume as Paradise Regained, Milton offers a poem of Samson Agonistes. To make a story short, after some peregrinations, everyone has a big party, and the final line is: And of calm mind, all passions spent.
> Scratching the itch can give you relief. Sometimes the itch comes back.

**Aging has advantages.** It's better to retire at an age where some of the pivotal moments are behind you: getting married, having kids, getting divorce. The surest way to gain some maturity is to gain experience by simply living through ups and downs. Passions abate as you age.

**Estimate spending rate.** If you don't want to ratchet down your lifestyle in retirement, your current spending rate plus travel and experiences budget can serve as the basis for retirement needs.

## 5.1.2 Steady state

During most of retirement, you will be on auto-pilot. I follow the buffer strategy. I continue to under-spend my limit and gradually simplify my life. It's advisable to keep the plan simple, allowing for wider margins to minimize the number of assumptions.

**Spending.** First, I estimate my spending rate to be about $100k. Here is a rough budget:

| Category | Annually |
|---|---|
| Rent | $24k |
| Insurance | $6k |
| Food and living | $24k |
| Travel | $30k |
| Spending shocks | $12k |
| Total | $96k |

About half to two thirds of that belongs to essentials. I could hold off travel and some one-time spending and save $30k to $40k. Using a basis of $100k is convenient, because every $1k of spending is worth 1% of total spend for the year.

**Total net worth at retirement.** I estimated a safe withdrawal rate at around 3%. That means that the total net worth at retirement need to be between $3M to $3.6M. I retired slightly short of $3M. This was a risky decision.

**Buffer portfolio.** We covered the buffer strategy. The sample assumptions in the Finance chapter are the same. The allocation is reproduced here:

|  | % of total | Value |
|---|---:|---:|
| Total portfolio | 100% | $3m |
| Yearly spend | 3% | $90k |
| 8 years of cash reserves | $8 \times 3\% = 24\%$ | $720k |
| Investable portfolio | 76% | $2.28m |
|  | Yield | Value |
| Dividend yield | $2\% \;/\; 76\% = 2.6\%$ | $60k |
|  | % of total | Return |
| Yield on cash | 24% | 0% |
| Total return on non-cash | 76% | 4% |

**Risk reward.** As Warren Buffett commented on the fall of the hedge fund Long Term Capital Management, don't risk what you can't afford to lose for something you don't need. It's fine to reserve some amount of excess capital to interesting endeavors, as fine as it is to spend it on an ornate sculpture for your living room. But don't touch the core portfolio.

## 5.1.3 Where we are in 2023

First, let's think about the proverbial arc of history.

**Generational shift.** It's a cliché that older people believe that younger generations are feckless and illiterate. I am no exception. Generally speaking, we are seeing the rise of a generation that was born and raised in relative prosperity and does not understand the causal relationship between work and wealth. It is fated to squander resources, taking them, by force, from those who have saved.

**Socialism and populism.** Without a doubt, we're entering an era of Big Government. It's hard to tell these days who intervenes more in the economy between China and the United States. That only goes in one direction: the rise of graft, increased expropriation and wasted resources. I estimate that we will be in this cycle for a decade.

**Civil liberties.** Starting with the Patriot Act in 2001, we have started to erode civil liberties in the West in leaps and bounds. During covid-19 we have enacted mass house arrests, wholesale shut down businesses, frozen bank accounts, denied citizens re-entry into their own country, and more. The Woke movement destroyed lives without due process, effectively abolishing *habeas corpus*, a legal restraint that we held dear for centuries. Within hours, you could be out of a job for inappropriate things you may or may not have done decades ago. Spying on citizens is routine in China. All governments agree to exchange information. It's always a good practice to keep a low profile, as if McCarthy was coming back into office next week. I don't expect we will ever return to a time when you could live off the grid unless, well, there is a total breakdown of civilization.

**Demographics.** South Korea has a birth rate below one, less than half the replacement rate. Many other countries also lack sufficient immigration to replenish their population. Economists complain when the population keeps growing and when it shrinks. On the whole, a leveling of population in an environment of declining or negative productivity is not a bad idea. It does mean that promises of assistance in old age, made by most advanced economies, will have to be reneged. It was immoral to promise what could not be fulfilled, and to raid the coffers of reserves all along.

**Credit.** The price of money will probably return to

## 5.1. FINANCE

its historical rate of approximately 5%. It is likely that the United States will experience periods of elevated inflation, then a Japan-like stagnation. I am hoping that we can keep it together, without hyper-inflation, social unrest and regime change. The transition of Europe from colonial power to open air museum was relatively painless, compared to the disorderly dissolution of the Roman Empire.

**Thucydides' trap.** We had a period when the United States was the sole uncontested military and economic hegemon in the world. That position is clearly weakening. However, I don't believe that the contender, China, will be in a position to supplant the US in the top position in the next decade or two. The quality of the political leaders in China is miles, miles above the United States. They have bad debt, a military and technology disadvantage, a geographical disadvantage, a demographic issue. Tensions will rise but I don't anticipate a scenario where the United States will suddenly be subjugated by China militarily or economically.

> **The pessimists.** During the cold war in East Germany (under Soviet rule), people joked that optimists learned the Russian language, while the pessimists learned Mandarin Chinese. Guess who won.

**Cold War II.** What we're entering, though, is a period of bifurcation, like we had in the Cold War. It's unfortunate and wasteful. It means that we have to split the world in two and restrict our ability to move and trade with half the world. I don't expect a open direct armed conflict between the United States and China in my lifetime, but it is far from impossible. It is arguable that a Cold War has already commenced.

**Happy times.** Love or hate the Pax Americana, the post Cold War era was a happy one, at least in the West. Interestingly, the period from the 1950s to the 1970s was also pretty good, all things considered. We exited the World War, a massive destruction of resources that ended the Great Powers. We had high inflation in the seventies. We lived through a cold war. We also faced the Savings and Loans crisis. It was manageable.

**Taiwan.** I reckon that President Xi Jinping is intent on seizing Taiwan in his lifetime. I don't believe that it will happen in the next decade. Since I am likely to outlive him, I will most probably see Taiwan come under communist rule in my lifetime. I just hope it happens in the least painful way for everyone involved.

**Energy transition.** The full cost of renewable energy, including mining materials, water for maintenance, environmental damage, shows that it is not a perfect source. We cannot store energy, and are unlikely to find a solution that doesn't involve a whole lot of mining. While they are relatively cheap, they don't provide base load power. For that, nuclear power seems to be the solution. We have the solutions, but not the ideology to do it. Prior to the war in Ukraine, Germany spent more than half a trillion on energy without curbing emissions. Her dependency on Russian oil was ill-advised. During the first winter of the war, she spent, again, more than half a trillion keeping her citizen warm with natural gas and coal, outbidding poorer countries for natural gas. The United States is likely to waste a couple of trillion dollars and waste at least half a

## 5.1. FINANCE

decade in ill-conceived policy, but eventually, she will avert a disaster.

> **Charlie Munger: I have a rule for politicians: it's a stoic rule. I always reflect that they are never so bad you don't live to want them back.** After the Gettysburg address, the Chicago Tribune published its assessment: "by the side of it, mediocrity looked sublime". Today, we are left to long for the bygone days when politicians could be counted on to be merely incompetent.

**Politicians.** In an era of expanded government role in every aspect of our lives, the quality of the decision making at the top matters. The Chinese Communist Party appears to have a system that tends to surface more competent leaders near the top. It is my expectation that governance all across the world will fare consistently in the lowest range of possibilities in the next decade or two.

### 5.1.4 Armageddon

Outside of the regular schedule, I'm expecting one big event. We're not talking 50% drawdown in the stock market, or losing electricity for two weeks, but a rather more severe issue that could leave my ability to live on passive income curtailed permanently. Given my current lack of preparedness, you may call me reckless.

**False alarms.** You don't want to risk a situation like being trapped in North Korea after the communist rule. Sometimes you'll have to take preemptive action. And sometimes it'll be for naught. I aim for a ratio of 1:3 or 1:2. I expect to fully gear up for Armageddon two to three times in the remainder of my life, and to be right once.

**Home goals.** In most countries, the chances of a foreign invasion are small. Most likely, you will lose assets (and life) in two - ways: a breakdown in enforcement of property, and seizure through expropriation from your own government. I monitor the situation closely. It feels like the boiling of the frog.

**Hold a Third World passport.** Large powers have coalitions. Right now, it seems like you're with the West or in the company of autocratic regimes. It might be that holding a passport in one of the blocks might be a liability in the other block. It could range from travel restrictions, heightened scrutiny, to arrest and confiscation of assets. If you don't have one, consider obtaining an innocuous passport from a non-aligned country. I hold a passport from Switzerland. Think about Russian or Chinese persons who don't believe in their own governments. They stash their wealth in Western countries, only to have it frozen when tensions escalate, resulting from the actions of the very governments they oppose.

**Keep a bank and brokerage account in another jurisdiction.** Opening a bank account and brokerage account can take a long time. Make sure you have a place to wire your money out of the country. Switzerland and Singapore have a rule of law that make it relatively safe to park your assets (and person) for a while. They have a tradition of good stewardship of property.

**Physical gold.** It's prudent to hold about 1kg of physical gold, or about $50k. Before you pay me a midnight visit, I don't have gold at home. Note that gold is neither a currency, nor a monetary instrument. It shouldn't be subject to capital controls or tax on cash. That isn't to say that government can break the law when convenient.

**Big white blocks.** If you go to the Alhambra in Southern Spain, you will find the palaces of the Muslim upper class pre-1492. On the exterior, they are bland. Inside, they boast luxurious architecture. There is a prohibition against ostentation in the Islamic religion. You would do well to follow that precept.

**Keep a low profile.** When it's time for the pitchforks or neighborhood vigilantes to act, they will come for those who stand out first. Jews, gays, aristocrats, gypsies, you name it. I eschew displays of wealth and political views in particular. The fewer people who associate my name to a group of any kind, the better. As an immigrant, I will always be a default target. I live in Puerto Rico, where there is a movement called "Gringo go home", which is a plea that is exactly like it sounds. I have been embraced by everyone I have met here, but you only need a small group of people that get radicalized to be unsafe. A single person can destroy many lives.

**Local community.** It's best to nurture good relationships with members of your local community. It will protect you from becoming a target of the mob. They are a network of people that you can rely on to substitute for infrastructure. Generally speaking, it's also more pleasant this way.

**Always be ready to move.** It's best to have a portfolio with liquid assets. There could be situations where you decide to move your financial home in as little as a couple of weeks. Be ready.

**Maximize resilience.** In order to maximizes your chances of success, you should find opportunities to live a frugal life. Simplify your life and enjoy simple pleasures. At the very least, minimize the core spending. Don't live in a house that is unnecessarily lavish, or define yourself as the one throwing the biggest parties on the block.

### 5.1.5 Legacy

The nature of compounding means that your money will either grow exponentially or you will run out of money. It is unlikely that it would end, perchance, near zero. In most cases and on expectation, you should die with significant financial resources.

If you plan on giving away your money to someone other than your government, you should prepare in advance. Tax law regarding bequeathal changes frequently. You should start planning at least a decade ahead and monitor the situation yearly for new opportunities.

I don't have a plan for legacy. That is, I plan for the remainder of my assets to be distributed to the youngest surviving family members, after the full inheritance tax has been forfeited to the State.

It is possible that I will use the legacy money in a *quid pro quo* transaction with an individual, family or otherwise, in exchange for support in the last stages of my life when I become severely incapacitated.

I plan on simplifying financial structures closer towards the end. Medical directives have been communicated. Physical assets will be disposed of. In other words, I plan to have a simple cleanup procedure.

## 5.2 Health

When it comes to health, I have tried many protocols, diets, and supplements. It is not clear whether treatments will apply to other people. The routine is probably going to change over the years.

**Yoga.** After an initial burst, I find that 20 minutes every other day to be adequate for basic maintenance. I train for flexibility, which I am sorely lacking, balance, and core strength.

**Walking.** I walk 8,000 steps per day, in about 40 minutes, on the beach, split into morning and afternoon sessions. I listen to audiobooks at 2.5x speed.

**Meditation.** I meditate between 30 min to 2 hours per day.

**Nutrition.** I eat a low-carb, quasi-ketogenic diet. While I would like to reduce meat intake, I have meat once a day. I avoid products with added sugar. I also eschew rice, potatoes, pasta, bread and other high-carb foods. I grow my own greens with hydroponics without pesticides and preservatives.

**Fasting.** I eat twice a day, around 9AM and 4PM. A few times a year, I will do a 3 to 5 day water fast.

## 5.3 Purpose

Now that I have all the time in the world to become a World of Warcraft world-class player, what do I do all day?

### 5.3.1 Goal

So, I want to live a life worth living. That will make me really happy. As you shall see, the converse is always true: to make me truly happy is a worthwhile goal. I am assuming that you have read and understood the contents of the chapter on **Purpose**.

**Impact.** As the word implies, impact means some effect on something. Ultimately, that something is the mind of people. You could solve Fermat's theorem in a handful of lines, if no one is there to see the proof, there is no impact. We shall accept that humans feel pleasure and pain, and minimizing pain and maximizing pleasure is in the right direction. There are many ways to do that. If I invented a way to solve the energy problem, that would be worthwhile.

**Maximize my impact.** There are numerous opportunities around me, and some match my talent and abilities. I could write poems, but they wouldn't be very good, at least initially. Only a few would read them, and yet fewer would enjoy them.

**Make money.** When you work, you add value. You help build a product that people want. In return, they pay the company for that, and the company rewards its employee to build the next product. At a high level and on average, this works. Google search adds 10 IQ points

## 5.3. PURPOSE

to two thirds of the world's population (say). It saved lives. That's true on aggregate, but when you talk about hundreds of thousands of employees, your own value add is less clear. Even as the CEO. This is why I retired: it was less clear how I added value, and I found a better way.

**Possible and verifiable.** So, while I'd love to make cold fusion possible, realistically speaking, it's not possible. Moreover, I'd like to have the most direct link possible to the production of value so that I can verify, here and now, that my contribution is appreciated. Again, if you measure impact in terms of incremental added happiness, it's hard to verify. (See the story in "Half The Sky" in the Purpose bibliography, where they rescue a woman from bondage.) Generally speaking, the closer you are to providing relief, the more certain you can be that you are making an impact. Few would argue that providing food and shelter is a good idea. Sadly, charitable organizations tend to be inefficient and occasionally corrupt.

**Beware of good intentions alone.** Under the leadership of Chairman Mao and Zhou Enlai, reforms led to excess death of tens of millions, by the Party's own reckoning, and probably in the 40 million range. They had good intentions and potential for high impact. You can control your intentions, but you have to have a minimum of wisdom to assess their consequences.

**All have equal value.** Because you can't measure impact with certainty, you should refrain from ethical accounting. You have to assume that all lives are equal, and that all acts of kindness are mostly equal. Should you kill a serial killer? A bloody dictator? Destroy someone's life to make a hundred million people laugh for a few seconds?

**Reasonable goal with tangible results.** It's better to start with a small goal and work my way up. Once I understand how to measure and obtain results, I can iterate from there.

**Start with one: me.** There is one special person in the world: me. This is only one person whose happiness I can measure with certainty. Of all people, the mind over which I have most agency is my own. There is the double advantage that if my goal is to make myself happy first, then if I succeed I will have helped one person and made myself happy in one swoop. And let's be honest: I only ever truly cared about one person: me.

**Is that selfish?** Let's go back to ethical accounting. Let's say you make one other person happy, while at the same time making yourself miserable. Because you are both equal, then you will have added no happiness on balance. So, you should only help another person if it makes you incrementally not completely miserable. But if you start with yourself, you already have full credit, and there's no trade-off to be made.

**No downside.** Again, because it's hard to compare happiness across people, it's hard to say that an action that will make me 10% less happy for two other people 10% more happy. Therefore, it's best to look for win-wins where making me happy makes other people happy. At least, the best is to find ways to increase your own happiness. That is the only true happiness that you can rely on to be true. At a certain point, it naturally comes by helping others.

**Multiple lives.** If you believe in Buddhist rebirth, then intentional actions in this life have an impact over multiple lives. So many, in fact, that it dwarves the num-

## 5.3. PURPOSE

ber of people you can help in this life. That's another reason not to use ethical accounting. Moreover, it gives you leverage and a longer time horizon for your investments to pay off.

**Purify my mind.** I believe that Buddhism has the best understanding of the human psychology of happiness. The doctrine provides plausible explanations for the causal relationships that govern the mind. It also provides a recipe to gently purify the mind towards happiness.

**Core teachings.** There are many schools, sects, and subtly different recensions of the basic texts that have emerged over the millennia. Then there are different translations. I follow teachers in the Thai and Burmese schools, particularly the Thai Forest Tradition of Ajahn Mun. I find Bhikkhu Bodhi's translations to be the best. There are a few technical terms for which you need to develop your meaning; Bhikkhu Bodhi is consistent so it's easy to re-translate the technical terms mentally.

**Simple life.** The path naturally leads to living a simple, happy life. In practice, the simpler life also means that you need less from your environment. Resilience makes your financial and health planning easier.

**Harmlessness and kindness.** The gift of harmlessness and kindness to oneself and others is the lowest hanging fruit. If you live a simple life, it is a natural disposition of mind that will bring you and others happiness. That is an achievable proximate goal.

### 5.3.2 Process

It sounds trite, but becoming happy is a mental transformation. To neuro-scientists, neuro-plasticity is a new thing. What isn't obvious is that it can be done intentionally. Buddhism provides the tools to do that in the so-called Fourth Noble Truth, the Eightfold Path.

> **Just as the great ocean has one taste, the taste of salt, so also this teaching and discipline has one taste: the taste of liberation.** During his roughly 40-year teaching career, the Buddha was accompanied by attendants. In the last 20 years, Ānanda was his attendant, known for his prodigious memory. The basic canonical texts consist of more than 10,000 teachings. There are numerous approaches and situations that lead to liberation. They are all consistent and converge to the same outcome. This is why there are many teachers and books today that attempt to reify the advice to your specific situation from different angles. Just as there are NP-hard problems that are equally hard, there are equivalent ways to describe Enlightenment. Simply begin with the one that resonates with you the most.

We are unaccustomed to observing and guiding mental processes. We'll have to learn how to do so.

**How it works.** At a basic level, to purify our minds efficiently, we need to first be able to monitor change. That is mindfulness. Then, we need to free our minds from automatic reactions such as addictions. They happen with

## 5.3. PURPOSE

apparent inevitability even if we can see them unfolding before our eyes. Once we have the freedom of choice, we can build new habits that are beneficial.

**Mindfulness.** In Buddhism, the original sin is ignorance, not biting the apple of Knowledge. Mindfulness is the initially fleeting ability to observe our mind as experience (feeling), emotions, and thoughts follow their course. To understand the chain of dependent origination is to comprehend the Buddhist doctrine, an equivalent to Enlightenment.

**Incline the mind.** If you understand cause and effect, it's easier to apply effort upstream. The earlier you detect the precursors of anger, the easier it gets to nip it in the bud. Setting up situations and conditions for a happy mind is gentle, upstream approach to mental transformation.

**Experiment and learn.** Meditation is like a laboratory with controlled conditions where you can experiment and observe mental phenomena without distractions. This is where you get closest to your optimal state. You can develop skills and habits that you can later transfer to your daily life. It's also a sobering wake up call to see how much of a slave to your mind and body you are: they can't wait for even a full 30 minutes.

**Things we know to be true.** Without experimentation and deliberation, it's obvious that certain mental postures are congruent with a happier life. First, live a simple life free from complications. Initially, that means physical isolation. Later, you can isolate your mind from harmful emotions while still engaging with the world. Maintaining an attitude of kindness at all times can only help. Resilience (equanimity) stems from accepting reality as it really is at all times. They are safe to practice at any time. You can't overdo it.

**Tracking progress.** You need to progress on two fronts: mindfulness and happiness. Without mindfulness, it's as if you're sleep-walking through life. Happiness resembles a subtle flavor in a soup at a Michelin-star restaurant. The more you experience it, the more you come to recognize it for what it truly is. It takes practice.

**Study.** There are many entry points to the Buddhist doctrine. Personally, I was first attracted by the theory of dependent origination. There are many lists to choose from. Unlocking the meaning is like understanding the demonstration of a theorem. There is immense satisfaction and a permanent quantum of progress. At the very least, you will not be cultivating old harmful habits. It is a way to frame your mind to a positive foundation.

**Pace yourself.** Purifying your mind is a lot like getting rid of addictions. It's relatively easy to apply yourself for a couple of hours, but if you want results to last for years and decades, you have to work on cutting the causes little by little at a time. If you rush, you will not achieve lasting results.

### 5.3.3 Schedule

We haven't talked about how to allocate time between finance, health, and purpose.

Here's how I spend my time on a typical good day:

## 5.3. PURPOSE

| Activity | Time | Duration |
|---|---|---|
| Waking up | 7AM | 30 min |
| Yoga | 7:30AM | 30 min |
| Walk on the beach | 8AM | 30 min |
| Cooking, eating and, clean up | 8:30AM | 1h30 |
| Meditation | 10AM | 1h |
| Main activity | 11AM | 2h |
| Cooking, eating, and clean up | 2:30PM | 1h30 |
| Walk on the beach | 4:00PM | 30 min |
| Main activity (2) | 4:30PM | 1h |
| Light activity | 5:30 | 2h |
| Winding down | 8PM | 1h30m |
| Bed time | 10PM | - |
| Main activity | - | 4h - 5h |
| Total reading time | - | 1h - 2h |
| Total meditation time | - | 45m - 2h |
| Total exercise (yoga, walk) | - | 1h |
| Total cooking time | - | 1h |
| Total sleep | - | 7h-9h |
| Total wasted | - | 2h |

There are days when I spend no time in the main activity - I just vegetate in front of YouTube, go to the movies, or fix one thing or another in my apartment.

Health is probably the least important. I want to do the bare minimum, but it still consumes approximately two hours of my day, plus the additional time to cook healthy. I listed up to 2h of meditation, but that's rare. On most days, I dedicate considerably less time to it.

Finance should be mostly on-demand. On most days, you read about news and update your view of the world slowly. But as Vladimir Lenin once stated, during those weeks when decades happen, it's going to be all consuming.

Ideally, I would slowly replace dead time with meditation. It has the triple benefit of being pleasant, working towards purpose, and resting the mind so that the rest of the day is more productive.

## 5.4 Retrospective

I wanted to write this book in retirement. It took three years to get to it. So far, the journey has been mostly within expectations. I moved to Puerto Rico.

### 5.4.1 Unexpected consequences

The lack of a secure cash-flow was something that was harder to get used to.

**Access to credit.** To get credit cards, you need to have an income. Banks require statements of a salary. It doesn't matter what your net worth is, the approval officer just doesn't understand the concept of a multi-million dollar portfolio backing a multi-thousand line of credit. I tried and failed to secure a local credit card in Puerto Rico. Apparently they don't run credit checks.

**Rental application.** Landlords want to see that you have a secure income to pay the rent. In that case, the process is more flexible. They also rely on credit checks.

**Self-employment.** It's likely that I might create a business so that I can pay myself. It will allow me to have IRA contributions and social security. Also, in this environment, it's better to be a net debtor. It's safer to house the debt in a limited liability corporation.

**Same life.** In many ways, it's surprising that my life hasn't changed all that much. Instead of devoting my waking hours to my technical passions, I spend my waking hours optimizing for a different goal.

**Off the beaten path.** Socially, it's immediately clear that the path of retirement at this age is off the beaten path. In America, when you meet someone, the protocol is to state your name and ask what the other person is doing in life, meaning, work. "I live a life of leisure" is an instant conversation killer.

**Anxiety.** I don't think about it explicitly very often, but a residual background anxiety is silently gnawing at me. In ten years, I might look back at my decision to retire as a momentous blunder of epic proportions. Retirement is still the decision that I choose rationally, mind you, but there's no denying that I could have miscalculated.

## 5.4.2 Finance

I retired in November 2019. I was slightly shy of my $3M goal, but close enough. For the first few months, I was slowly re-arranging finances and simply resting. Then covid-19 happened. Biological events were at the top of my list of events to watch out for. However, I failed to realize that governments would seize the chance to destroy small businesses, the heart of economic activity, to combat what appeared to be a nasty flu. It is estimated that a trillion dollar was embezzled in the USA alone. My portfolio was down 15%. Again, I misjudged the speed at which dollars flowed from the fiscal and monetary stimuli to the asset markets. I missed most of the recovery.

**Give me chastity and continence, but not yet.** My goal is to implement a simpler rational portfolio with index funds. Somehow, it seems that a big crisis is always just around the corner. I keep a portfolio of individual stocks, ETFs, and bonds, with a large portion in money markets. I run a proprietary quant trading system with a small amount but relatively large proportion of total volatility. It's hard to give up control even though a two decades of relative under-performance should be a strong clue.

I was somewhat shaken by the experience. While a downdraft of 15% was expected, it's not a pleasant thing to happen. It's 5 years of my annual allowance, or 10% to 20% of total retirement years. Starting in May, I started working on quantitative trading techniques. Starting in September, I followed a slow ramp up of investments to half a million dollars. I kept the system running at full speed until March 2021. At that stage I had moved a quarter billion dollars. The system required discretionary decisions, and starting in February, it was starting to exhibit enormous intra-day volatility. I kept the system running throughout 2022 at a loss. On balance, after tax, the system added a few years of runway.

In 2021, Washington State started to get real on capital gains tax. A new administration at the White House made it clear that more mismanagement of economic resources and expropriation was on the way.

I had a long-standing dream of moving to Thailand, a tropical country with friendly, tolerant, and honest people, excellent mangoes, coconuts, and some of the best Buddhist temples anywhere. I couldn't decide whether to become an American citizen or give up my permanent residency (and incur immediate capital gains taxes on retirement accounts). Instead, I moved to Puerto Rico, a tropical land with friendly people in the Caribbean. It is a US territory. As such, it is a tropical island for beginners. As an incorporated state, it has dominion over its tax collection, so I am partially insulated from changes in the mainland until the statute expires in 2035. So far, financially, it's been a net loss of a few years, though. Moving overseas meant that I had to dispose of moving boxes that I had kept with me for 20 years. It was an emotionally difficult but ultimately liberating experience.

Living on a lower budget is a challenge. Getting used to being thrifty increases resilience.

| Year | Outlay |
|------|--------|
| 2020 | $88k |
| 2021 | $79k |
| 2022 | $69k |
| 2023 | $82k (estimated) |

On the whole, it seems that I am able to live within my budget. After decades of profligacy, I am becoming a little neurotic about restraining my spending.

### 5.4.3 Milestones

In retrospect, it might be a good idea to establish a few milestones along the path to punctuate your advance. It serves to acknowledge the progress you have made and frame how the future might look like. It has to be done in a way that doesn't bring stress and become a goal in its own right. It's too easy to confuse the scale with the thing itself.

**Time-based.** The first kind should be time-based. Every few years, you should check in with yourself. Evaluate how you are doing in terms of finance, health, and purpose. You should also set an expectation in where you are, in terms of crises weathered and aging, for instance.

**Five years.** I estimate that the first five year mark to trigger the first existential soul searching. Many people would choose to alter their view then. They might choose to return to work, get divorce, or re-orient the purpose they pursue.

> **You can name a price or a date, but not both.** Economists have long understood the key to making accurate predictions. It's hard to tell when things happen, and much stress arises from aligning results over a pre-ordained timeline.

**Triggered.** The second kind of milestone is trigger-based. You set a target and you achieve it in whatever time it takes.

### 5.4.4 Tyranny of lists

During the planning phase, I was mostly interested in having the confidence that my estimations were correct. During the implementation phase, I only had a vague idea of what to do. I'm still working on it, slowly.

## 5.4. RETROSPECTIVE

I am gradually accumulating lists. Lists are a good candidate for streamlining operations. Moreover, they are also easy to find and edit at that random time of the day when you think about something. The downside is that they tend to be on an external solution which requires manual steps to execute. Make sure the software allows for offline operation on your smartphone.

**Meta.** There are interesting findings about how we react under stress, and one thing is for sure: we tend to do stupid things. Lists tell us what we should do without the pressure, and hashing it down for efficient execution. What scenarios do we need to prepare for? Right, we need a list for that.

**4-hour list.** There is a tsunami warning. You have four hours to vacate. Decide immediately whether to hit the road, or you might die in a traffic jam. What do you pack? How do you secure what you left behind? Whom do you contact? Where do you go? Do you have an AM radio?

**Line of business.** What items or services do you need to perform daily operations? Cell phone? Car? Laptop? Email services? Prescription glasses? Medications? Make sure you have backup options or reserves. You can start with your travel packing list.

**Moving money.** Now it's time to move your financial home. Do you have a plan to move your assets? Do you need to give instructions to your correspondent bank? Are there fees involved? Can you retain tax-advantaged status of your retirement savings? Is there a substitute for FDIC/SPIC insurance? Is your broker in sound financial condition, and is there an institution that could take over the administration if there is a problem?

**Shelter-in-place.** I live in Puerto Rico, where Hurricane Maria left the island without power for months. What if I had to shelter in place? Do I have food, enough gas to cook, water filtration, ammunition, and the like?

**Restructuring asset base.** There is a major change in the geopolitical situation that requires a major rebalance, say towards commodities or fixed income. What is the target allocation? Which specific bonds or securities? What are the tax consequences? Who is the custodial? Do you understand the covenants of the debt issuance?

**Final cleanup.** You have been diagnosed with cancer. It's time to say your goodbyes. What etiquette do you have to follow? Financial moves? Is your will and medical directive in order? Did you leave a mess in your house? Any last prayers?

## 5.5 Epilogue

Congratulations, you've made it to the final section of this book! Thank you for following me so far.

**Behavioral monetarist.** Irving Fisher introduced the use of "real", to mean inflation-adjusted in our lexicon. In the introduction of his 1928 book, "The Money Illusion", he apologizes for revisiting, yet again, the monetarist theory. He argued that people did not adjust to a larger money stock because they were fooled by nominal prices. He called for a "scientific approach". We introduced precise mathematics, but sacrificed faithfulness to reality at the altar. Today, MMT – magic money tree or modern monetary theory – stipulates that money stock doesn't matter, you can fool all people all of the time.

You may think that most of this book is just common sense. Guilty as charged. To my defense, we have touched on topics where common sense has been obscured by too much thinking. Retirement planning is rooted on three disciplines that have regressed in the last 50 to 100 years: economics, nutrition, and psychology. It is hard to verify or falsify a theory because it is challenging to make a direct observation. And so it is today that people continue to argue about the causes for the Great Depression. We still don't recognize sugar as the addictive, harmful drug that it is. Hypnotism (then called Mesmerism) is largely ignored today, because it's rare and difficult to observe - contrast that with supra-conductivity in electricity, a rare phenomenon that breaks conventional operation. (No progress is not always negative: Theravāda Buddhism, by choice, remains the same as it was 2500 years ago.)

I hope we were able to cut through the mess. This book can be read in a day, although it might leave you with homework for the rest of your life. I have taken a common-sense approach with down to earth examples. We have to admit that there are basic quantities that we don't know – as fundamental as future returns on stock investments.

This book was written for the prospective DIY retiree. We present mental frameworks for approaching this seemingly daunting topic. There are no ready-made solutions: no one should trust anyone when it comes to making the most important decision in their life. Furthermore, retiring early presents the challenge of sustainability more acutely. Something that is merely possible in a decade becomes as good as certain over half a century. After you use these mental tools to construct your plan, you should know if you are ready to wave the first chapter of your life goodbye.

The first aspect to cover is securing material resources, specifically **finance**. We recognize that bad things can happen – so bad that you could lose your savings and your life. You can categorize them and identify a structural temporal pattern. For the rest of the time, we looked at how classical financial planning works: project spending, calculate required savings by estimating a withdrawal rate, and portfolio allocation. While they rely on fundamentally flawed assumptions that minimize the risk, they are still a good starting point. We briefly go through the properties of fat tail distributions, which govern financial asset returns, which more or less invalidate the possibility to give too precise a number on future expect returns. Among asset classes, equities are the most advantageous since they represent a share of a productive business. We present the buffer strategy as a means to weather storms: rely on a savings buffer and a dividend income stream to endure a 16-year trough.

The second aspect to cover is staying alive and in good **health**. I differentiate between longevity, which cannot be extended much, and healthspan, which is the number of years of enjoyable healthy life. The goal is the latter: maintain a body that will allow you to move with grace and dignity for the rest of your life, however long that

## 5.5. EPILOGUE

might be. If history is any guide, it would be foolhardy to expect medical advances to stem or reverse the tide of decay of your bodily functions. To keep my body and mind healthy, I center my efforts on sleep, nutrition, and physical training. I use mental clarity as a guide. Unfortunately, it is difficult to get a clear understanding of what truly works, so, for the most part, you'll have to experiment on your own.

The final aspect to cover is **purpose**, or living a life worth living. We questioned the false dichotomy between duty and pleasure. We equated happiness and a life worth living. We brought more clarity on what that means, over time and on your last breath. To find a suitable goal, we gave a few desirable properties, it should be sustainable, unconditioned, good for self and others, attainable with continuous improvement, and be the highest calling. We couch these properties in the technical language of the Buddhist doctrine.

I've applied these concepts to my situation. My master plan consists of accumulating \$3M and spending \$100k per year, preparing for Armageddon and always being ready for a 16-year trough. My daily body and mind hygiene consists of some meditation, yoga, walking, and eating a diversified low-carb diet. All the while, I am training my mind to live a happy, simple life guided by Buddhist principles.

The mental tools presented here are just that: tools that you are free to use or discard. You may use them and come to different conclusions. There's absolutely no one you can trust when it comes to perhaps the most important decision in your life. My goal in this book is to pre-hash the space so that you would know to ask the right questions.

Think the long game, and watch for the down side.

Now it's your turn to write the next chapter. Go forth and conquer! I wish you a happy rest of your life.